Breaking BUSY

FINDING PEACE IN THE CHAOS

Linda Edgecombe

MOtivational PRESS®

LEADERS IN GLOBAL PUBLISHING

Published by Motivational Press, Inc.
7777 N Wickham Rd, # 12-247
Melbourne, FL 32940
www.MotivationalPress.com

Manufactured in the United States of America.

ISBN: 978-1-62865-117-1

CONTENTS

FOREWORD 5

PROLOGUE *Super Man and Wonder Woman* 7

SECTION 1: How Did We Become this Busy Culture? 9

   CHAPTER 1 *Holy Crap I'm Busy!* 11

   CHAPTER 2 *Trailblazing the Time Crunch* 16

   CHAPTER 3 *Our Current State: The Busy Audit* 19

   CHAPTER 4 *The Way We Do Things* 23

   CHAPTER 5 *Waiting on The Big Payday: The Pros and Cons of Being Busy* 26

   CHAPTER 6 *The Great Distraction: Clutter* 29

   CHAPTER 7 *What Fuels Our Chaotic Norm?* 32

   CHAPTER 8 *Identifying Your Busy Personality* 36

SECTION 2: Putting the Brakes on Busy 41

   CHAPTER 9 *Being in Control is Totally Overrated!* 43

   CHAPTER 10 *Listening to the Ache of Exhaustion* 47

   CHAPTER 11 *Unpacking the Weight: Deciding What Holds*
               True Value in Our Lives 50

   CHAPTER 12 *Embracing the Environment We're In* 53

   CHAPTER 13 *Disconnect to Re-Engage and Notice What You Notice* ... 56

   CHAPTER 14 *An Attempt to Kind-a Disconnect and Sort-a Re-Engage* ... 59

   CHAPTER 15 *Rest Up and Clear the Chatter* 62

   CHAPTER 16 *Our Decisions Aren't Made in a Vacuum* ... 65

   CHAPTER 17 *The Silent Company of Loneliness* 68

   CHAPTER 18 *Exposing the Truths of Vulnerability* 72

   CHAPTER 19 *Nothing But Time: An Unexpected Silent Retreat* ... 75

   CHAPTER 20 *The Elusive Search for Happiness* 79

   CHAPTER 21 *Even if You Don't Walk The Camino, You Still Walk A Camino* ... 83

SECTION 3: Finding Peace in the Chaos 87

   CHAPTER 22 *What Do You REALLY Want?* 89

   CHAPTER 23 *The Fearless Leap: Going After What We Really Want* ... 95

   CHAPTER 24 *Change 1: The Organized Buy-In* 98

   CHAPTER 25 *Change 2: Becoming Selectively Indebted* ... 101

CHAPTER 26 *Change 3: Increasing Fitness and Overall Health* *105*

CHAPTER 27 *Change 4: Put-Offs Quickly Become Off-Putting* *109*

CHAPTER 28 *Change 5: Reducing Stress* *112*

CHAPTER 29 *Change 6: Cutting Back on Negative Influences in Your Life* *115*

CHAPTER 30 *Change 7: Throwing Guilt Down the Gutter:*
You Might be a Martyr if… *118*

CHAPTER 31 *Change 8: What To Do When Satisfaction Isn't Guaranteed* *123*

CHAPTER 32 *Change 9: Balanced Living: The Classic Dilemma Between*
the Head and the Heart *125*

CHAPTER 33 *Change 10: Self-Awareness: Getting to Know Me Better* *130*

CHAPTER 34 *Change 11: Why Kindness is Highly Underrated* *134*

CHAPTER 35 *Finding Peace in the Chaos* *137*

ABOUT AUTHOR *140*

FOREWORD

It was my intention to have someone , well known, who has really shaped my thinking, values and outlook on life to write a foreword for my book. I just never thought everyone who is on that list would be so busy. So instead I just want to give a shout out to the various cool and interesting people who I admire because I am who I am because of your ideas, and contributions to the planet. I was very impressed that Gloria Steinem's office actually wrote me back to say she was busy, but Brene' Brown, Tim Ferris and my favorite sassy woman Jann Arden, I didn't get a yes or a no. So, if your life gets a bit less busy and you want to write something for the 2nd edition of Breaking Busy, I will be here for you.

On a more serious gesture, I need to thank my family for supporting me in finding a slower gear in my life and my awesome girlfriends who I treasure more everyday I grow a bit wiser.

From a more literary perspective, my niece Kristen Bounds for helping me with some of my research and to Joscelyn Duffy, my writing coach, and editor. You are one talented lady who kept me on task and added so much to the process and richness to writing this book

PROLOGUE

Super Man and Wonder Woman

From the outside looking in, you would think that my husband and I are *Super Man* and *Wonder Woman*. We are both business owners - Kevin owns and runs a very busy commercial and residential development company in the Okanagan Valley and I am a motivational speaker and author of several books. We have two teenage daughters, seventeen and twenty, two dogs, one cat and a fish, who simply refuses to die. For the past nine years, we owned a hobby farm that was full of fruit trees and seven acres of grass to mow. I travel on average six to ten days a month and have been doing so for twenty-four years. On top of all that, we both have big families with aging parents, who we try to see and keep in touch with regularly. Oh yes, and then there's the fact that we are both regular fundraisers for a charity called IWEN (Inter-cultural Women's Educational Network), where we rescue girls in Nepal from child contract labor. I'm tired just telling you all this, though here's why I am....

This inside scoop into our busy lives isn't so that you can say "Wow! How do you do it?" That is the kind of feedback that has fed our egos and what has gotten us here, living the "Busy Life" in the first place. I'm being this transparent with you because I want you to know the whole story. I want you to know that in many ways, you and I are perhaps not all that different.

While we've had our share of great business opportunities and memorable moments, the past two years have also been brutal for our family. Kevin had a critical accident at work, which took him literally off his feet for three straight months. We sold our farm (his soul) and got rid of dozens of truckloads of "stuff" just to fit into an average size home, where we now live. And through financial pressures, family illness, etc, etc, Kevin and I had to re-visit why and how we will be together as a couple moving forward.

A year ago, I decided to get more curious about how we had arrived at this place - this point of being so "Busy" and having neglected to question so much along the way. I started asking friends, colleagues, my entire database and readers: *Why has BUSY become the norm of our generation?* I mean, our parents weren't like this and their parents were definitely not like this.

As leading offenders and as the poster family for the "Busy Culture," I decided that it was time we "*Broke Busy* and found some peace in the chaos."

I wrote this book because I had totally created and bought into my life as a very Busy Person. I realized that even as a humorist, who makes people laugh for a living, I was experiencing a strong sense of deep unhappiness in my own life. Somewhere along the way, our generation has "lost our way." We've forgotten to listen to the voice within us that continues to try and direct us to happiness and we've bought into what have become our cultural norms. Coming into the realization of what we've created for ourselves, I was determined to figure out how we got here, find out how to break that cycle and offer adoptable changes to take the exit ramp off the Busy highway and create a life that aligns with what we *really* want.

I hope you are as curious as I am. So, if you're ready, let's get started.

Yours in peace and happiness,

Linda Edgecombe

How Did We Become this Busy Culture?

CHAPTER 1

Holy Crap I'm Busy!

Breaking Busy: It's time to sell your shares in the "Deferred Life Plan."

Sometimes the obvious teacher smacks us right in the face. As I walked into Starbucks and waited in line for my Joe, I found *him*. As I worked to tie together all of my thoughts, opinions and research about how we've gotten to this "Busy Life" and how we can "Break it," there he was: my poster child (or at least one outside of me or my husband). I couldn't help but notice and overhear him, sitting in the table in the corner, loud enough for the entire staff and guests to hear. In the fifteen minutes I stood in line and shared a conversation with a friend, he has been on the phone with three different people, all of whom he's had a conversation with about what needs to get done *today*. What time the air conditioning technician would be at his house. How and what his assistant could do to prepare for the upcoming meeting. What his wife had to get from the grocery store in order to prepare dinner. I watched him take each of these calls while frantically working away on his laptop, on what looked like a mass of charts from my vantage point. Watching him, I thought: add in kids' schedules, taxi service, the dog's vet appointment, an hour of exercise (if we're lucky), that one extra work project, and ten more calls to coworkers and your spouse, and you've got the epitome of "Busy." Maybe some of this is sounding familiar?

And just like my Starbucks poster child, you may not even have the slightest idea that you've even been sucked into this "Busy Culture," this vortex of Busy. All you know is that you feel drained and far from fully satisfied. Something's missing and you don't even (think you) have time to figure out what.

When did this all start? When did we get so busy that we've literally left ourselves no time for ourselves? How did we get on the fast track to somewhere so far from genuine happiness?

Let's start by getting real about our individual circumstances. Where do you find yourself on the "Busy Scale"? Do you know if it's time to take the off ramp on your busy *life is a highway*? Here's an easy way to find out:

A Personal Assessment

Answer "Yes" or "No" to the following questions:

1. Do you work full time?
2. Do you have a part-time job or business too?
3. Are you finding you are working extra hours or have to commute most days?
4. Have you lost that loving feeling for your work lately?
5. Do you have children?
6. Are your children in out of school activities?
7. Do you fundraise for your children's activities?
8. Are you in a relationship?
9. Have you been on a date with your partner in the past month?
10. Do you have extended family that you see monthly?
11. Do you manage people in your workplace?
12. Do you own a home?
13. Do you have pets?
14. If you have a lawn to cut, does it take you longer than 1hour/week to complete?
15. Do you have one or more spaces in your home that need to be de-cluttered?

16. Are you eating out of your house more than at home lately?

17. Are you finding time to do the things you love to do outside of your career? Are you losing things your normally don't? Keys, wallets, cell phones?

18. Are you waking up most days feeling tired?

19. Have you been easily frustrated or angry at insignificant things?

20. Do you have a low level sense of 'unhappiness' lately?

Count the number of Yes's and the number of No's. If you answered yes to SIX OR MORE of the above, then I invite you to join me and **BREAK BUSY.**

Let's cut right to the point. I decided to conduct a *Busy Audit* survey and according to the results, those of you right in the middle of life's craziness (ages thirty-six to forty-five) are generally the most unhappy about **one or more** things in your life. You need change, but A) don't know where to start and B) are afraid of the risks that any type of change could bring. This inaction results in a subconscious effort to keep "Busy" and avoid life's mounting clutter (you know, that "stuff" that is flooding your mind and taking up every square inch of your home and/or office).

Going "I don't know how it got that way, it just happened." This statement says a lot about society's general assumption of not knowing how something happened, because you and everyone else around you were "too busy" to notice. What we don't really realize is that just because we have a million things on the go, it doesn't mean that what's coming out of it are good, quality results. Quality over Quantity, always. In this case especially, less is more.

"Life is what happens when we are busy making other plans."
– John Lennon

In the article "Productivity and Happiness: Why Are We So Busy?" Lori Deschene writes, "*Our obsession with productivity is partially a reflection on our beliefs of the North American Dream: the idea that our potential for happiness is intricately tied to our freedom to pursue wealth.*"

We have grown up to believe that *Success = Happiness*, and Deschene proves a valid point when she states, "*Busy didn't make me feel happy, but it created the illusion that I was somehow building a foundation for that feeling someday, somewhere, when I could finally slow down and be free.*"

I call this living on the **Deferred Life Plan:** waiting until something more or better comes along and then, we will kick in and start to do what we really want to do.

"If Money Was No Object, Everybody Including You Would Be Doing This"
- Anna Chui

Let's be real. When you ask, "What do I really want?" what are the first things that come to mind?

To answer the **"What do you really want?"** question is interesting because I really only know a handful of people who have actually pursued their dream job and are genuinely happy with their decision to do so. If it were true that money were no object, we would be a lot happier. We would also consider ourselves more successful solely on the fact that we *knew* what we loved to do and pursued it. The feeling of creating a goal for yourself and achieving that goal might just be the best feeling out there. People have this idea that being busy and constantly having your plate full with activities, work and distractions will eventually lead to being that person you've always wanted to be. We've forgotten that time moves faster than even we do when we're busily juggling work life, home life and all the clutter in between.

I believe that we all want to be *both* successful *and* happy. However, in the process of striving for both and being unclear as to how to attain them together, we end up being too busy for either one. Our "Busyness" and "Clutter" becomes our idea of how to realize and accomplish what we really want. We're lost somewhere in the deep woods unable to see the trees for the forest. ...Or at least that is what we believe and what becomes our excuse for not being and doing exactly what we want.

CHAPTER 2

Trailblazing the Time Crunch

Breaking Busy: We are the innovators of running through life on a gerbil wheel and the noise the wheel makes is driving us crazy!

My twenty-one year old niece, Kristen, has a really nice way of putting what has become of our generation: "Thinking back to that project my teacher made me do in kindergarten, asking what I wanted to be when I grew up, I sure as hell didn't write, 'I want to be a full-time mom, taxi-driver, wife, worker and people pleaser.' Five-year-old me would not be impressed."

"With that being said, as you get older, you grow, reality sets in, media plays its roll, people influence you, and eventually, the goals you once had growing up aren't as 'important,' because you have a family to provide for, a job that requires your full-time attention, a mortgage, student loans and clutter that just won't seem to go away. You're in way over your head and you don't know how you got here. How did you let life slip away from you like that?"

The way we've been brought up has a massive influence on how we see life.

We are the first generation to buy into the "Culture of Busy." We could arguably stake claim on this as one of our most influential creations, though not necessarily a wholly beneficial one.

Baby Boomers (born 1946-1964) grew up with the mentality that anything is possible and worked hard to get to where they are today.

Most were educated as well, which automatically set them up with opportunities.

The one thing Boomers, especially the **early** ones, did *not* do was 'helicopter over' their own kids.

My parents were born in the late 1930s and my sisters, brother and I were born between 1957 and 1965. My parents never drove us *anywhere*. If we wanted to get somewhere, we either biked, bussed or walked. End of story. We only became involved in sports and activities that we could get to *by ourselves*. Life was about knowing that I had to be home by the time the streetlights came on. Where I was and what I was doing was really not a concern to my parents.

We all became independent in an age that was economically affordable and we left home as soon as we could. Many of us had kids and went on to breed the next generation.

Some of us Boomers had Generation X kids (born 1965-1979) and some of you are Generation X kids. You were the first generation to be exposed to more media, good and bad. Given this, you've developed a skeptic characteristic, making you more independent in the workplace and in life in general. But as far as parents go, you also became nervous and paranoid of what could happen to your own kids and are all too competitive about how your kids measured up with other kids. You got your kids into more and more activities, so that they too would have the 'upper hand' in life.

If you grew up in this generation, you know how very full your "Busy Plate" is and how many of you have taken on larger mortgages and financial burdens in an increasingly challenging economy (which is just another addition to your endless work pressures). And oh yes, your kids are still at home, making your time for yourself very limited and it's not always the most relaxing.

Then, there's Generation Y (born 1980-2000). They have almost completely grown up with and were ceaselessly exposed to the Internet, mass media and technology. They've known and found comfort in diversity; and therefore, they expect it in the workforce. This generation of kids can't figure out why their parents won't just leave them alone. Will they ever stop hovering over you?

Most of you Generation Y kids have had a cell phone since you were in grade six. And you wonder why your parents get ticked off at you when you are texting during dinner. Your parents keep saying, "Look up from that thing when I am talking to you." You just want some freedom, but can't afford to be on your own with the cost of living being so very restrictive. Unfortunately, you have enjoyed the toys and lifestyle your parents have exposed you to and you can't afford to create it on your own, so you are staying at home for up to ten years longer than your parents did, which drives both you and your parents crazy.

With all this said, and regardless of which generation has shaped our choices to arrive where we are, we have become the trailblazers of the "Busy Culture." As naturally as taking on the cultural habits of generations past, we have simply created this and adopted it as our lifestyle. And while our Busyness has led to our endless pursuit of everything in life, it's time to step back and answer the question that transcends all generational differences: "Are we happy?"

Are you living a life and lifestyle that brings you joy and energizes you? Or, are you exhausted and run off your feet, round and round the gerbil wheel, not really seeing joy in much of your day to day experiences?

If we can step back and look at what got us here, in this state of relentless Busyness, in the first place, then we can drop some of the guilt about moving away from the cultural norm we first bought into. For your own sake, I encourage you to take a long hard look at how you want the next ten years of your life to unfold. We are raised being guided by the beliefs and habits of our generation, and then we reach the point where we alone get to decide how we want to live.

How do you want your life and happiness level to feel moving forward?

Our Current State: The Busy Audit

Breaking Busy: We've surrendered the helm to fear.

Many of you slowed down enough to take my *Busy Audit*, which further confirms just why we stay hovering in "Busy Lane."

I asked, "If you know there is a change you want to make in your life, what keeps you from making it?"

One thousand people surveyed, top three answers on the board:

1.   **Fear.** Not knowing the outcome, keeps me from making changes.

2.   **I don't have time.** My life is too full right now to even think about making more changes. (i.e. I am living in a world of clutter.)

3.   **I over-think** and need to plan before I make any changes. Need I say it again? There is fear of not knowing the outcome.

I am sure that the top responses in this survey aren't surprising to you. They may all fall into your reasons why change is not your favorite experience either.

In case you were wondering, money and relationships came in fourth and fifth as reasons why most people don't move on changes they know they should.

As you can see, according to the *Busy Audit*, we're allowing fear to rule our lives. One thing we do know is that most of us on the "busy treadmill" will say that our base level of general happiness is lacking or even nonexistent. And yet, we keep filling our lives with fear and worry, without consciously knowing that it's this clutter in our heads that is keeping us from finding happiness. Basically, we are creating a vicious circle of being busily unhappy. If that choice alone isn't enough to dizzy us or wear us out, add on the extra activities, taxi driving, fundraising for your kids programs, etc that you've added to your daily to-do list. We're keeping ourselves so Busy in a desperate attempt to reduce the strain of fear and avoid physical, environmental, mental, emotional and financial risk. And where has the "Standard of Busy" gotten us? More on that to come.

We're physically busy, mentally busy and emotionally drained. In spite of all of our efforts to steer ourselves away from fear-based stress, we feel overwhelmed, frustrated, resentful and simply unhappy.

But alas, we have all the power to choose to break the busy Cycle, if we really want to. That's coming in Section 3 of the book, as we look at what we can do about these top reasons we stay "hovering in fear." But before we get *there*, let's take an even deeper look at what being *here*, in the "Busy Life," is doing to us, and just how the heck we got here.

Second up on the list of why we avoid change: "I don't have TIME. My life is too FULL."

What is it about the badge of honor that keeps us so busy?

There have been times in my life when I believed all my happiness revolved around how busy I was. If I was busy, I was using time wisely. If I was busy, I was proving to myself that I was valuable. If I had too much "down time," I thought I was lazy and could be doing something else. If I was busy, I was creating the possibility of a better life in the future and any threat to my productivity was a threat to my sense of hope. I was born in the 1960s. By the 1970s, I had bought into the whole woman's movement - I even became a card-carrying Gloria Steinem supporter. *You can do it all Linda; you can do it all.*

I received great feedback when I was moving all the time. This feedback made me feel valued and became how I defined myself.

We want to be deemed valuable and productive in today's society.

We want to be accepted and appreciated. We'll take on anything and everything to prove to people that we make a contribution. The badge of honor is our lapel, our calling out to the world, wanting to prove to people that we are worthy and valuable.

News flash! Only one part of us needs all of this reassurance and boosting: our egos. And it's all too easy to get caught up in ego's importance of "Being Busy."

Those of us who know that we have bought into the "Busy Culture" most likely know that we are constantly feeding our egos with the ongoing feedback everyone around us gives us. "Look at all the stuff you've got going on!" "I don't know how you do it all and keep on smiling!" "You amaze me!" I mean, look at yourself: You have a full time career and a small business on the side. You are building a new house or renovating the old one. You are coaching this team and that team and driving your kids here and there. Oh yeah, and then there's the constant fundraising, fundraising, fundraising. And then we can't figure out for the life of ourselves why we can't sleep well.

In Section 3, we'll really look at how you're spending your time. Until then, start to ponder this point: we all have the same number of hours in a day and we all have the choice of how we use them.

Now, if you're reading this and thinking, "Linda, I can't just get up and DO this, making big changes in my life. I over-think and need to plan before I make changes," reason number three on the *Busy Audit* is for you.

Regardless of your personality traits, those of you who are thinkers need to know that we are all motivated by our fears and the biggest fear for a thinker is making a mistake. You will do and re-do everything, just to avoid the possibility of making a mistake. Being out of control, or even appearing to be out of control, is a very uncomfortable situation for you. Decision-making is a laborious process in your (over-thinking) mind. What can I say, you love research and data. You ask, "Why is it not working this way?" and "What are my options?" The most spontaneous thing that may happen to you is a hot flash; and I'm sure you have remedies ready to go at arm's reach. The thought of surprises literally causes tension in your stomach, so you have carved a life that is calmly predictable. And that is just fine.

But here's the catch: life is messy. Shit happens almost daily, adding some bumps or foot-deep potholes to your nicely carved out road. You have either found a way to deal with the daily changes or you avoid them all together, but I'm going to propose something new: Before you can get your mind to take a break from incessant thinking, you have to make friends with it. If you try to tell your mind to go away or that you don't need it, it will just work harder to control you. Such is the power of our ego mind.

The only way to end our "Busy cycle" and unconscious hovering through life is to take a long hard look inside of our minds, at what we've created for ourselves and about what we REALLY WANT.

CHAPTER 4

The Way We Do Things

Breaking Busy: We're wearing ourselves out, running from "What ifs."

Cul·ture (ˈkəlCHər) *noun*: The arts and other manifestations of human intellectual achievement regarded collectively.

Simply put, "Culture is the way we do things around here."

The "Culture of Busy" that we have created has become the benchmark of success, or at least the appearance of success, for anyone between the ages of thirty-five to sixty-five. Even if you're retired, you better be doing something good for someone somewhere in the world. Don't get me wrong, being productive and contributing to the planet is not what I am harping on about here. I'm talking about taking on so much stuff and filling every second of our days with Busyness to the point of being unable to find space to breath, let along figure out what it is you really would *like* to be pursuing - what really makes you happy.

We have created a treadmill of "Busy," rapidly driving us through our days and long into our "retirement" years. Many of us don't even realize we are on it, let alone know how to get off. We just think that this is just "the way we do things around here"...in our Busy Culture.

Culture is behind almost everything you do, think and feel. Without us even realizing it, our cultural norms are subconsciously incorporated into our lives as we grow up. And by the time we're in the workforce, choosing a life partner and starting a family, they have already become a major part of who we are and what our core values and morals are. Busy has become what we subconsciously expect of ourselves and of others -

that's what we believe our culture has dictated. We judge each other on it, without logically (or compassionately) thinking about it.

How did we arrive at these cultural norms? What drives our infatuation with Being Busy?

My thoughts are that it all originates in fear. The *Busy Audit* survey results support this. You've said that fear is keeping you from achieving your dreams. Why is that?

I was fifteen years old when my dad finally broke down and got cable TV. It was about the same time he got us a colored television. They had been around for a while, but he's just stubborn about stuff like that.

What instantly happened when cable shined into our living rooms was that we went from two Canadian channels to dozens of channels with mostly American, with a few more Canadian shows thrown in. Instead of hearing the news at 6pm and at 11pm, we watched morning news, news at noon, the 6pm news and the 11pm nightcap (soon to become the 10pm news as more people were still awake then).

With access to "all news, all the time" came all the not so positive or hopeful influx of things that were going on in the world. If we turn on our televisions or browse the web, we are subjected to the news. So let's cut to the chase and be real with who we've become: we've became afraid.

We live by the "**What If?**" factor. Cable TV and that color television brought to life a whole new world for us as kids. When we sat around watching four newscasts a day (let alone one!), we started to allow fear to feed how we lived our lives. And that fear, which had so unconsciously crept in, spread like an out-of-control weed when we, the former *freedom kids* of the Baby Boomer generation, started having kids of our own. Our kids then started spending way more time inside because those "what ifs" drove us all indoors and we, as parents, felt the need to supervise *everything.*

We send our kids to school long before kindergarten because four years old isn't early enough. Our two year olds are learning a second language and taking self-defense lessons, just to protect themselves on the playground. And oh yeah, we drove them there and picked them up.

Fast forward, past the microwave, computer, email and cell phone to a life of "instant everything." In person and electronically, we are overloaded with the images of what keeps us fearful. It has become our new cultural norm. It's pretty darn hard to be happy when we're scared 24/7.

So what does any of this have to do with being Busy?

CHAPTER 5

Waiting on The Big Payday: The Pros and Cons of Being Busy

Breaking Busy: Busyness can breed productivity and purpose, along with inflexibility, exhaustion and unpreparedness.

It's time to take a closer look at what our Busy lifestyle of running from the "What Ifs" is doing to us.

We all know when an accident happens, traffic almost comes to a halt so that we can stop and watch it. And the only news that sells is negative news. From an energetic point of view, the reason we are drawn to the negative, as much as we are drawn to the positive, is because there is energy attached to it. We are drawn to it for the sheer fact that we want to connect.

There are much happier ways to connect. We have to consciously make a decision to not see the graphic images and pull ourselves away from the negative scenes, if we want off this Busy treadmill.

Some of you may say, if I'm not Busy or keeping up on (negative) news, what am I going to talk about with my colleagues at work? How often we look at someone who has painted a room full of artwork or has already gotten in a eighty rounds of golf or sixty days of skiing this year. We think, "Well, someone's sure has a lot of time on their hands." *Must be nice,* we think. We think of it critically, instead of a lifestyle choice. Do we ever stop to question whether "that person" is living within their value systems? At a deeper level, are we not just outwardly expressing our own desires and resentment, which is a reflection of what we think about ourselves? Maybe we're identifying a (positive) point about which we could *truly connect.* Of course, asking "that person" about how and why they live as they do might just lead us to make the choice about whether or not to change...

Why do we, the human 'species,' so often stay with what we know, even if it is slowly killing us inside? Because we fear. We fear change. It is filled with "What Ifs!"

In his Lifehacker.com article "Why You're So Afraid Of Change (And What You Can Do About It)," Adam Dachis says, "What we don't know tends to scare us, and change creates a lot of things we don't know. As a result, we tend to act pretty irrationally to try and prevent change, often without realizing it, and make our lives unnecessarily problematic."

How many of us keep busy doing predictable work and activities? We do what we know and know what we do. We do it the way we've always done it, day in and day out. We create and collect on end, filling our lives with extra things, activities, positions, titles, etc, in an attempt to ensure that we maintain our "Busy lives" and the sense of purpose and security they (seem to) provide. That's the perceived upside of being Busy.

While Busyness leads many of us to have pursued careers that contribute to fulfilling a purpose in our lives, many of us are really only doing what we feel we have to. We have jobs that we believe will keep us employed for decades and leave us with a nice pension to retire on. We think that "Being Busy" will provide us with security and maybe it will. Maybe.

Here's the deal: the fear we have about all the "what ifs" is food for our egos. It pushes us further and further down "hover line" toward a life of being Busy, without allowing us a moment to question, let alone initiate any kind of change or heart-based decision making. Fear is in the driver's seat. And in our state of "not having time" to do anything about it, we're not standing back to see that our chronic over-thinking about our daily decisions and those frightening "what ifs" is our ego driving us right to where our fear is telling it to go. Our ego becomes fear's chauffeur and we're sitting in the back seat, along for the ride.

Here's the downside to our Busy lives: As much as we sit in the back seat and think we've found security in our Busyness, life still happens. We face unexpected job cuts, family crisis or financial strain—the "what ifs" that we thought our Busyness would keep us from ever having to face. We have to deal with them, already feeling emotionally drained from the impact of our Busy lives.

We have a hard time focusing and wrapping our head around the stuff that really matters because we've overburdened our minds with fearful thoughts and endless to-do lists. And we haven't a clue how to take a moment to ourselves to digest real crisis on a deep level. We don't know how because in spite of our being pulled in a million different directions in our everyday lives, we've actually become rather inflexible. We know what we know and do what we do, rarely questioning much outside of that.

So, all the while keeping so Busy, thinking that we're doing good, doing exactly what we "should" be doing (what our cultural norm suggests we do), it takes our facing something unexpected, something more real than our everyday Busyness, for us to realize that our lifestyle, while seemingly productive, is also rather problematic. We are Busy and we are stuck like gerbils on enclosed wheels.

It's time to venture outside of what we know and maybe even slow down, just a little.

CHAPTER 6

The Great Distraction: Clutter

Breaking Busy: We've proudly built a colossal kingdom
of clutter.

With our minds overwhelmed and days packed full, what do we do? We bring in more stuff. Why? We have created these Busy Lives filled with physical, environment, mental, emotional and spiritual clutter because more clutter makes us *look* busier and more important. We also love clutter because it keeps us from having to deal with what we really want. You know that calling from deep within you that tells you there is something else you want to be doing or somewhere else you'd rather be? That voice that won't go away no matter how much you try (to do everything other than what it is asking you to do). That's the voice of what we really want - the low muffle that can *almost* be heard from beneath the giant pile of stuff that we created on top of it, in our attempt to drown it out.

I have always been a believer that everything serves us in some way; otherwise, we would do something about it. Whatever clutter you are keeping, collecting or just ignoring serves a purpose to some part of you. And for that, I invite you first and foremost to honor it. Realize that it has served you in some shape or form and then sit with it, feel it and **breathe**. If it energizes you, keep it. If not, wish it farewell and thank it for what it has brought you.

Kelley Whitis wrote an article called "Clearing The Clutter," in which she asks, "Why do we keep so much stuff? You know, the stuff we'll save for later, wear when we're skinnier, read later, re-gift later, use again, or put up next year for the holidays even when its broken and we swear we'll get it fixed before then. Plain old clutter?"

Physical clutter makes us feel busy. There's a lot of stuff around you, so you must have a lot going on, right? Maybe. The truth is that holding onto keeps us feeling heavy, weighed down and not necessarily happier. It takes up a tremendous amount of room, even if metaphorically, where new opportunities could arise or new changes could set in.

Kelley goes on to say that "Clearing out the emotional clutter was so much harder than the physical. And trust me, it's not pretty. Which is why I'm sure it's easier for us to ignore the emotional clutter than to dig through it and get rid of what's not serving us. Pain hurts and it's our natural human instinct to avoid getting hurt."

When we're so caught up in our Busy Lives, we truly don't feel as though we have time to go through our "emotional clutter." There aren't even a few minutes in the day to get your mind back in tune with your body by meditating, crying, journaling or just healing yourself. And so, we're left feeling even more weighted and burdened, carrying around way more than we want or need to and leaving little room in our lives for new.

Clutter is self-created fuel for Busyness. Our homes and minds have become a reflection of what we experience in our jobs and hear on the news every day: a giant mound of overwhelming stuff that we have to find our way through. Stuff that makes us feel like we have a lot going on, when all it is really doing is making us feel more overwhelmed, not to mention, further away from that crying of our heart's desires buried deep under the pile of stuff.

Ask yourself, do you stay late at work because you feel you need to or because it's the easier option for you (versus going home and dealing with life there)? Do you continuously re-decorate your home as your creative outlet, knowing you really don't need four new throw pillows and matching candles? Or how about all those magazines you subscribe to and that "someday" you will get to cutting out those recipes and maybe, just maybe, prepare one. Facing ourselves is simple but difficult, because as I said before, it's not easy to admit that we all have faults. We are all flawed and just being present with ourselves can be uncomfortable at first. When was the last time you tried starring in a mirror for a good few hours? OK minutes? That's what I'm talking about: starting to REALLY get to know ourselves and why we do the things we do… or the things we don't do.

Here's the thing. All of this physical and emotional clutter, while overwhelming, keeps us "safe," or so we think. We think that it keeps us from that frightening need to face the continuous messages from within us - the voice of what we *really* want to be doing.

An April 2009 article by *Body+Soul* called "Clear Your Clutter, Find Your Life" says it best: "…I help people figure out not only what they want most, but what they need to let go of to discover who they really are. To do this, I use what I like to call the 'Michelangelo method,' based on a story about the famous sculptor. Legend has it that when Michelangelo finished the statue of David, a local patron of the arts, awestruck by the work, asked how he did it. The artist responded simply, 'David was always there in the marble. I just took away everything that was not David.'"

What if we gave ourselves permission to de-clutter and let go of some of our stuff? What if we allowed ourselves to live a little more fearlessly, turning off the news and tuning into that calling from within us? What if we grew strong enough to gently say "No"? Would our lives then become a little less burdened? A little less Busy? How would we even know where to start?

I suggest we start by taking a good hard look at what is keeping us buried in this place of deep unhappiness.

CHAPTER 7

What Fuels Our Chaotic Norm?

Breaking Busy: We're giving our Busy Lives an unenthusiastic "Yes."

So here we are: we're chronically Busy, emotionally exhausted, and buried deep in a massive pile of clutter, attempting to run from the fear of "what ifs." And the biggest kicker of all: we're not even happy doing it. All of our Busyness is making us unhappy over-thinkers with nothing left to give.

Our generation has lost that lovin' feeling. We've forgotten what use to make us laugh and just simply smile. We've forgotten to base our days around what nurtures our spirits. And if you are honest with yourself, you haven't said "You know what guys, it doesn't get any better than this" in you can't remember how long.

There's a minority population that truly intrigues most of us Busy folks and they are the "Happy People." These are the people who have found a way to "balance their Busyness" and be strategic in dedicating most of their time to what makes them happy.

What differentiates them from the rest of us? What are we doing that they aren't (or vice versa), which is leading us to fuel our chaotic norm? And what keeps the rest of us from becoming more like them?

Let's take a deeper look into the lives of "the Happy People."

Firstly, happy people focus on what they *do have* as opposed to unhappy people, who only focus on what they *don't have*. Focusing solely on what you don't have only brings out the negative parts of your life, creating stress and more chaos.

Secondly, happy people lead somewhat balanced lives and have made time to focus on what they love, be it their family, friends, career, etc. They can be just as Busy as everyone else, but they're conscious as to the choices they are making in their Busy days. Unhappy people tend to already have a lot of "clutter" in their lives and when something bad happens, it's just another addition to the list of things to worry and stress about (i.e. even more chaos). There's no apparent space or time to deal with anything other than the demands of their Busy everyday lives. The exact same things happen to happy and unhappy people, yet happy people simply understand that bad things happen sometimes and that they have the time and patience to deal with them.

Thirdly, happy people have found what they're looking for, and spend their time doing what they love. Most importantly, they know what they want, so they can say "No" to what they *don't* want. This is what differentiates the happy from the unhappy the most and what fiercely fuels our chaotic norm.

When many of us say "No," we're saying it from a wholly different perspective from the happy population. We aren't saying it by conscious choice to pursue what we truly want to do, but rather because being busy has become the easiest way to 'get out' of doing things. We say "No" because our plates are simply too full - full of stuff that isn't what we really want to be doing. It's much easier for us to get out of things because we are SO busy, than it is to say "No" appropriately in the first place.

Lord knows we want the rest of the world to love us; so saying "Yes" has been the flagship to feeling good about ourselves and becoming more like those Happy People (when in fact, we are eating ourselves up inside with resentment for being asked and saying "Yes" in the first place).

Most of us think the world won't like us if we say "No," which is far from the truth. People who ask for favors will usually move onto the next person and ask them, and all the while, you are sitting and worrying about what they are thinking about you. News flash: most people aren't thinking about anyone but themselves! Simply put, happy people know how to say "No" to the things they don't want to do and move on, without worrying about what anyone thinks. Those who don't yet know how, sit and worry what would become of us saying "No," or silently get mad at the person who asked them in the first place. And then, we get madder for saying "Yes" at all… or we make "I'd love to, but I'm so busy" their new "No."

Our inability to say "No" in the first place is like throwing butane into a fire. We're swamped at work and we say "Yes" to the additional project that our boss needs done yesterday. Our evening has not much more than a second to spare, but we say "Yes" to baking those cookies for the fundraiser. We're wondering how to make financial ends meet this month, but we really can't say "No" to that charity we support every year. We're busily unhappy and we take on more of what we don't truly want to be doing, thereby making us unhappier… and Busier. We are fueling our chaos because we aren't taking the time to question what it is we truly want to be happy and dedicating our "Yes's" and time there.

Would we appreciate our jobs, activities, positions and opportunities to help others more if we selectively chose only those we truly wanted to do? Could we then find a little extra happiness in doing each of them, knowing that we made the conscious choice to say "Yes"? If so, then the question becomes: what keeps us living this "Busy Life" if it's not bringing us real happiness?

Now don't let this quick look in the mirror get you down. There is hope and I will lead you down the off-ramp of busy in the last section of this book, but we really need to take a good look at what got us here. Truthfully, we come by "Busy" honestly and we've put a lot of effort into getting here.

The next chapter is our start; our chance to take a moment and really question who we've become and what kind of life we've created. We'll define our "Busy Personality."

In order to change parts of our "Busy Life" into parts of that "Beautiful Life" we occasionally sit and daydream about having, we need to become aware of our own individual "Busy ways" and what they are doing to us. Then, we'll figure out just *what to do about them.*

CHAPTER 8

Identifying Your Busy Personality

Breaking Busy: We all have a unique intrinsic motivation for our Busyness.

In over twenty-four years of working with people from around the globe, one thing I have observed is that although we are different, we are definitely predictable. This is where most of our humor comes from: being able to relate to the foolish things we all do.

While we are each unique, we do tend to fall into four basic "Busy Personalities." Read over the following and see if you can find yourself in one of these. Sure, you may fall into more than one, but which one is most predominant? And what traits resonate with you?

When it comes to how busy we have become and how we react to these situations, we tend to fall into one or two of the following personality trait patterns:

1. Hurry Ups: Look at you walk and talk fast. Everything you do is quick and you have zero patience for folks who like to take their time with anything. You cram as much as you possibly can into as much time as you've got. You start projects and never finish them. You have energy and are usually never late. But you're also never early because that would be a colossal waste of time ten extra minutes that you could be doing something else with. You walk the planet with a sense of unease in your gut. And if you don't already have enough chaos in your life, you will subconsciously create more.

Who am I kidding? You don't have time to read anymore. You know who you are.

2. Pleasers: You lovely people pleasers, you. Seriously, you make the world a better place to be. You simply never say "No" to anyone or anything. You like being helpful and the thought of someone thinking poorly of you is simply not acceptable to you. Your biggest fear is not being included and what gives you the greatest turmoil is a lack of recognition for all the stuff that you do daily. "Yes" is the name on the flag you wave, until the day when you blow up from all the "stuff" you have taken on and no one can figure out why you are so upset (which makes you even madder because you think they should be able to *see* all the work you have taken on). Fortunately or unfortunately, you have created a passive-aggressive way of communicating. Believe me, when you say "Yes" to one more thing on your overflowing plate, you make a little mental note and intend on pulling that tidbit of info out down the road when you need it to ensure everyone is pleased with all you do.

3. Perfects: What could we ever say about you Perfects? You are perfect after all or at least that's what it looks like on the surface. Regardless of what you have going on, you certainly know how to pull yourself together. I'll bet right now, if you have not already made a few notes on some of my grammatical errors that you will send to me later, I will bet that your underwear is matching your outfit. And why wouldn't it! From a full busy plate perspective, taking on tasks that you know you can't execute perfectly is not an option for you. They have to match your standards, just like how your underwear does with your outfit.

What "Busy" has created for perfectionist is a less-than-rich experience in the general sense of life. Messy is not a word in your wheelhouse. Trying something for the sake of trying something makes absolutely no sense to you. You have a high need to be in control or at least appear to be so. And if you do take on an extra task, the stress you cause yourself trying to make the outcome perfect is so high that it basically causes you to back off. So ironically, perfectionists are not really that busy.

You can be lonely and not as fulfilled as your heart may desire. The crazy thing about perfection is that even perfectionists know that perfection does not exist.

There are two kinds of perfectionists. The first type are folks who have a really high standard for themselves. The second kind are people who have really high standards for themselves, along with everyone else around them. If you are number two, then you go through life constantly disappointed because life is a messy ride. The rest of us are guaranteed to disappoint you.

4.   **Popeyes:** Well Popeyes (and only you Boomers will remember Popeye!), you are the strong, not always so silent, types out there. Your plates are full because you have an incredible need to be in control of every situation. Instead of asking for or getting help on anything, you say to yourself, "If I give this away for someone else to do, they will probably mess it up and I'll have to do it over; so I might as well just do it alone and save myself some time."

The bottom line here is that you simply cannot do it all. Burnout is something Popeyes experience, along with all the stress that comes along with burnout. Popeyes live a lonely existence and because you never really work as a team member on anything, you become alienated. No one around you steps up anymore and why should they? You never accept help, delegate or allow others to take risks and failure. It's just not an option.

Creativity gets squashed when we try and do everything ourselves. You need space to be creative and there is none of it available for you "I can do it all" folks out there. Doing nothing is an uncomfortable activity for you, but for your health's sake, I want to encourage you to take it on for a day.

All in all, whatever you busy personality is, whether you are deep into one of the above or a blend of several, just be honest with yourself and ask:

"What are the parts of me that are really working and what parts would I like to move away from?" "What makes me smile and get energized from and what's draining me?" This is not rocket science, just plain honesty. You can be the only one who is the wiser. It's up to you.

Once you've gotten real with your busy ways, let's explore what this "Busy Life" is doing to us.

SECTION 2:

Putting the Brakes on Busy

CHAPTER 9

Being in Control is Totally Overrated!

Breaking Busy: If it hurts on every level, you'd better be asking yourself *why* you're doing it.

"You don't choose a life, you live one." Those words jumped out at me as I watched the trailer for the movie *The Way*, with Emilio Estevez and Martin Sheen, leading me to press the "Purchase this movie" button. That one click initiated a two and a half year obsession with the Camino and turned out to be an incredible platform to reveal the truths of what our Busy Lives are doing to us.

El Camino de Santiago de Compo Stella, or *The Way of St. James*, is a series of over eight hundred kilometers (nearly five hundred miles) of pilgrimage routes across northwestern Spain. In Christian tradition, the route was believed to be one on which plenary indulgence could be earned; in other words, those who traveled it would be removed of all punishment for sin. Believe it or not, this was *not* my main reason for wanting to go. However, after a tough year with homes, business and relationships, I figured I needed my own "coming to Jesus" moment. A big part of me knew that I needed to take on the trek, but I didn't yet know why. I didn't have a clue that the decision to go would be the start of one of my biggest game changers in my life to date.

In preparation, I relentlessly read, watched, listened to and Googled everything I could get my hands on about walking the Camino; and I searched out anyone who had walked or even thought about walking it. I planned, packed and exercised, day in and day out, in attempt to ready my physical body for walking the over eight-hundred kilometers in thirty-two days.

I also insisted that I go alone. No buddy, no girlfriend, and no husband. Doing so was my hardest decision…except perhaps opting to make the trek at a time of year when the rain, snow and wind were my ever-present company (more to come on that one).

On March 13th, 2014, I (over)packed my sixty-five liter backpack (which I quickly realized was a *big* mistake) strapped on my not-so-broken-in Gore-Tex boots and boarded the plane. Twenty hours later, I landed in Biarritz, France, where I took a shuttle van to St. Jean Pied Port. I was welcomed in through the miniscule wooden door of the quaint little Albergue (hostel) I'd call home for the night.

There, I sat alone in my room nervously thinking *Now what?* Even after two and a half years of preparation, I found myself in a foreign land feeling completely lost.

I arrived in France and Spain knowing only a few languages: English and "Cereal box French" - an offshoot of the French language available for study in Canada, where we have both English and French labeling on everything. (As a kid I learned the language through the comparison of the English and French details on the cereal box that was sitting in front of me at the kitchen table). In my adult life, I also mastered the art of "Bar Spanish": banyo, uno mas, cerveza por favor… You get my point.

In the northwestern part of France and Spain, they know only one language: *their own.* And so, I became adept in a fourth dialect: pointing. I simply got really good at pointing to what I needed.

Walking into the pilgrims' office, I officially signed up for the Camino walk, paid them the required eight Euros and took a picture of them stamping my passport. They told me that my trek begins by crossing a bridge out of town (or I should say, they pointed it out). Aside from a small guidebook to the rural countryside that I would travel, there were no further directions to show me "The Way." The office volunteers believed that everyone who came to the Camino was on a pilgrimage and apparently, pilgrims are able to find their own way.

At 7am the next morning (which was considered sleeping in by pilgrim standards), I pulled myself out of bed, still very much feeling the effects of the previous day's travels. I got dressed in my overpriced merino wool clothes and decided that I might as well begin my journey in an attempt to sweat out my jet lag.

Day one was the most physically demanding day of the entire trek: twenty-seven kilometers, straight up and over the Pyrenees mountains. It was extremely challenging, incredibly beautiful and filled with non-stop conversations with myself (some of the content is not repeatable). Over eight hours of walking and negotiating with myself that it took to complete that first day's uphill feat, I didn't see or speak to a single pilgrim...unless you account for the fact that I had become one.

Only seven hundred and ninety kilometers to go...

The first few days of the trek, while physically grueling, had involved me walking in picture-perfect blue skies, sunshine and twenty-five degree Celsius temperatures. And then, things drastically changed.

The rain and snow arrived on the third, fourth and fifth days. On day six, Mother Nature decided to throw in fifty kilometer per hour head winds. You know those swimming pools that create a current that you can swim against to build your physical strength? My journey became very much like being in one of those, every day, for eight straight hours.

I'd finish my twenty-five or thirty kilometers for the day and stop into the next Albergue that awaited me. I had been spoiled with a cozy hostel the first night and I was trying to adjust to progressively crappy accommodations from there on in. I did so while desperately attempting to dry out my soaking wet clothes, pad my daily blisters, manage Achilles flair ups and ACL inflammations and subdue mounting toe nail infections.

At first thought, the idea of sharing my sleeping quarters with twelve to twenty strange men seemed like fun; but who was I kidding? I was no longer in my twenties and the choir of snoring each night was a bit much. Comfort was no longer a word in my vocabulary and there wasn't really anything around that resembled it to point at anyway. And so, I just kept to myself, smiling and hoping to connect with someone at some point.

With six hundred and fifty kilometers to go, completing the trek seemed daunting. Every day exhausted me. I thought, as Shirley Valentine quoted in her movie of the same name, that I was going to feel all "lovely an' serene" on this "coming of age" trip, but instead, I just felt daft and old. Like Shirley, I also wanted to have a glass of wine in the country where the grapes were grown, which to my pleasant surprise, was cheaper than drinking water.

Even drinking cheap wine (alone, which isn't that much of a party), it was very tough for me most of the time. I began to dread everything and every day. With all those hours spent talking to myself (in increasingly non-repeatable terms), I start to wonder if how I felt was just how others felt when they had a job that they believed they *had* to go to every day? My decision to take what I thought would be a life-changing walk across France and Spain no longer felt like a vacation or the "finding myself" trip that I had hoped for. It felt like an exceedingly strenuous job that I had chosen to place myself squarely in the thick of. It was a sentiment that I had never felt before.

It was only day seven and already, I didn't want to get up in the morning.

CHAPTER 10

Listening to the Ache of Exhaustion

Breaking Busy: If it hurts, don't sit on it. Move on it!

No matter how many articles, blogs, documentaries, novels and stories I read during the two years prior to leaving for Spain, they all said the exact same thing about the Camino: expect a physically gruesome week, one mentally strenuous week, one emotionally taxing week and then finally "Your spirits lift and it all just seems to come together." And as much as I hate to be predictable or succumb to the norm, I should have expected to have an experience that was somewhat similar to most of the other pilgrims who have gone before me over the course of a few thousand years.

Peel back the layers and the progression of everyone's Camino experience unfolded in the same basic chronological order, touching the same five essential levels of our lives: the physical, environmental, mental, emotional and spiritual. But this general order of experience was the ONLY truth reflected in everything I had read, watched or listened to.

The images of smiling faces, the stories of profound insights gained and the freedom from all mental and emotional strain were not exactly how *my* Camino played out. Unfortunately, I had built up such an expectation of what my once-in-a-lifetime trek across Spain was *supposed to be* that when it wasn't so, I felt more alone. When was I going to have that "A-HA" moment, an epiphany or, at the very least, dry underwear?

So yes, the journey began with with physically painful first week. I had trained before I started my thirty-two day trek, thinking that hiking and walking every day for an hour or two for two straight years was enough.

Sadly, it wasn't. I'm not sure if there was really any way to prepare my body to know what it would be like to hike five to eight hours a day - day after day. Oh ya, and throw in an additional weight from an over-sized, excessively-packed backpack.

As I lugged around those extra twenty-seven pounds through grueling daily walks, the physical pain I endured would shift around my body. It started in my left knee, moved up to my hip flexors, and then down to my right Achilles, over to my left shin, and up to my shoulders, before I realized how sore my lower back had really become. And that's not to disregard the good number of 'hot spots' developing on my toes. In spite of all the unexpected factors of my trek, my story of physical pain was predictably much the same as everyone else's on the Camino.

Seven kilometers in for the day and just twenty more to go…

My physical pain wasn't much different than what is experienced by those who have bought into "the Busy life." The reason we hurt is because, through careful examination of our day-to-day routine, we spend a whole lot of time sitting! (Okay, so that part is a little different than walking for five to eight hours a day for thirty-two straight days, but bare with me because walking that much isn't realistic in our day-to-day lives anyway.)

For most of us, our work requires that we park ourselves in less than ergonomic office chairs and stare at a computer screen for the vast majority of the day. And when we're not sitting and working, we have a coffee break, go get a cup of Joe, and then sit down to enjoy it. We then either get something for lunch and eat it while sitting at our desks (because we are so busy) or we sit in a restaurant to eat. Carrying on with our day, we have meetings that require sometimes hours of just sitting, leading us right until the point where we go sit in our vehicles and commute home. By the time we've reached home, we might have twenty minutes to spare and long for nothing more than to hit the couch because we're so darn tired. Oh, but you're not finished sitting! It is then 'taxi time', where we've all bought into driving our children around to their various extracurricular activities. And when you finally get a moment to yourself at the end of the day, you spend it fathoming how nearly impossible it would be to fit any kind of physical activity into your busy life. If the exhaustion of it all wasn't enough, you then realize that every part of you has begun to hurt: your shoulders, hips, lower back, knees and even your ankles. They hurt because you are not moving them.

According to Health Canada, sitting has become as dangerous to our health as smoking. Scientific experts are now saying that if you are sitting for most of your waking hours, you are slowly killing yourself. The list of ailments caused by sitting is seemingly endless.

And yes, I realize that this is just one more 'thing' to add to your already overflowing plate of things to do, remember or make an all-out attempt to avoid.

The irony in my getting away from the 'pain of sitting' to walk across Spain is that it still took a couple of weeks until my body started to stop hurting. Most of us have spent years building up our current physical pain; it surely isn't going to disappear overnight. All we can do is start somewhere, surrendering some of our busyness for a little self-love.

Just when I thought I had overcome my own physical pain making my way over the rolling hills of the Camino and my legs and back became stronger, the pain then seemed to move…directly into my head. There I stayed, (un)comfortably seated 'in my head' for five to eight straight hours a day.

If you're nodding right now, then you're starting to see just how my Camino walk makes us even more alike. We're overtaxing our bodies and overstraining our minds on our endless treadmill of busyness.

CHAPTER 11

Unpacking the Weight: Deciding What Holds True Value in Our Lives

Breaking Busy: If it's weighing you down, ditch it!...
both physically and mentally.

We all know it and I have said it many times over the years: most of us will never really change anything until it gets loud enough or painful enough. And even then, we may or may not take a step back and change a small part of ourselves.

To fulfill my big need to manage my "comfort zone" on the Camino, I brought with me the most outrageous items. I started to call them my "just in case" items. I had just in case I get sick meds, just in case my knees, ankles or any other part of my body hurts athletic tapes, just in case my first four pairs of ear plugs get lost extra pair, just in case I see a bug of any sort spay, just in case my dorm smells tea light candles and a just in case the sun hit the earth survival kit. For those of your who have been to Spain, you are laughing because the one store you see the most of in Spanish towns is *Pharmacy's*. My pack was so large that I could have adopted a baby and brought one home in it.

After a week of torture, the pain in my hips was loud enough that I decided to walk one day without my pack. I took only water, along with my camera, passport and wallet. Now that day was an eye opener! It was like I was floating off of the ground! Nothing hurt, and I remember thinking to myself, *so this is what my body would feel like if I literally lost twenty-five plus pounds.*

Feeling newly-inspired, I decided to let go of some of my stuff. I packed up all extra clothes, leggings, long sleeved shirts, underwear, down filled vest, winter hat and mitts and mailed them home. I mean hell - it was twenty-four degrees out! Ironically, the one "just in case" thing I did not pack was sunscreen.

It was all of three days before the weather took a turn back to winter, and needless to say, I bought back a few of the items I had sent home.

Here's the reality: the late great George Carlin did a very funny sketch on why we humans have so much "Stuff." We keep things/stuff "just in case" (for those "What Ifs" that keep our minds so Busy and us so scared). "We keep stuff in our lives and responsibilities on our plates "just in case"." After all, we don't want to regret letting things go.

So whether you are collecting junk in a junk drawer, clothes from the 80's, memoires of volunteer positions for your kids' sports teams or old birthday cards, it's time to take note of your "just in case" stash. Are you truly going to sit down some day and look back through them?

We have to know that there's a cost to carrying all this "stuff" around with us all the time; and there is also a payoff, otherwise we'd let some of it go, immediately. As you work through this book, the key will be to figure out **why you keep busy** and **what it's doing for and to you.** If you really want to step off of the busy treadmill, then **getting rid of stuff** is mandatory. Our "Stuff" (Clutter) is weighing us down and stressing us out. It's adding to our chaos and holding us back from acknowledging what we really want. So not only is our clutter fuelling our "Busy Life," our Busy Life is leading us to create more clutter (for all the "What Ifs"). Are you dizzy yet?

As you begin to think about all the stuff that you've accumulated in your Busy Life that is no longer serving you, it's worthwhile to look at the other side of the coin: what do you truly cherish?

One night, as I lay awake listening to the various tones and pitches of snoring in my *dorm room*, I reflected on what items I really cherished on my Camino walk. If I could have only my seven most appreciated pieces in my pack, here's what they'd be:

1. My ultra light walking poles: They totally kept me going and were lifesavers in the mud.

2. My Marmot rain jacket: A very expensive investment that lived up to its worth keeping me warm in the wind and rain.

3. My Keen Gore-tex boots: Not once did my feet get wet in endless days of rain!

4. My I-pad Mini – I had bought it as a treat for myself, thinking that I would blog while I was on the trip. Instead, it was my portal to sanity, when I had *no one* to talk to for days on end.

5. My iPhone: It basically was my camera and link to the rock and roll anthem that pushed me through the last three days as I walked into Santiago.

6. Letters from both of my daughters, which they told me to read them when I felt that it was time. This one gesture from them is what got me to finishing this trip.

7. Notes from my girlfriends for everyday I was there. At the end of each day, I would sit down, order a cold beer and read their daily inspiration.

Oh and one more thing: Don't ever underestimate the power of a zip lock bag. Now that is one brilliant piece of equipment.

I would not have wanted to do any of this adventure without the above. What could you not take on your daily adventures without?

CHAPTER 12

Embracing the Environment We're In

Breaking Busy: If it's beyond your control, change your perception, creatively cope or can the complaining.

The second week of the Camino journey snails up on you. It feels like you have been walking for a year already, and then you realize that you have six hundred and thirty kilometers to go. My feet were getting calloused and some of my toenails were turning a gruesome hue of black (no polish required). On the Camino, you develop a "pain routine;" and just when you think you're pushing to the brink of your physical abilities, the wind picks up and the rain really starts to fall. And at higher altitudes, that rain turns into snow.

One day, about six hours into a head wind that made walking seem like attempting to make headway in chest-deep water all day long, a transport truck drove by me. Hitting the heavy very wet snow on the side of the road, it sprayed a filthy wash of cold, thick slush all over me. All I could do was yell, "Are you frick'n kidding me!" and then burst into a fit of laughter. There was no one else there to even see it happen - no one to laugh with, no shoulder to cry on. I wanted nothing more than to go home. I was hoping someone would call me up and say *just come home.* I was looking for any reason for an out: a problem in the office, someone who needed me at home, - anything!

Nobody called pleading for me to return. And so, I took a day off in

Logrono and enjoyed the city known for its Tapas bars, and then I pick up my heavily calloused feet and headed out again.

I had to figure out why I was having such a tough time. I mean, it's *just* a long walk across Spain. How many of us even get to do this? What a privilege it is to be able to afford this first off, and secondly, to have the luxury of thirty plus days to myself. My Grandma would be rolling her eyes at me right now. Perhaps many of you are. Yes, I am a princess and I have no idea what *hard* is. So as I sat trying to pull a backbone out of my spaghetti spine, I sent a message home to my cycling trainer Leah Goldstein. To prelude what Leah sent back to me, you have to know who Leah Goldstein is....

By age seventeen, Leah was the World Female Kickboxing Champion. By eighteen, she had enlisted in the Israeli army and was soon transferred and trained to become an Elite Undercover Commando Officer. When she left the Army, she took to cycling and won dozens of tours before taking to long distance riding. She won the longest (single stage) 5300 kilometer race called *Ride Across America*. Are you getting the picture?

So, when I sent her a text feeling sorry for myself at my *dinner for one*, set on an all-too-quiet rainy night, this is how she responded:

(Note: She swears in this, but she also knows how to get my attention)

"If you don't finish you will regret it forever!! You are doing something insane, something most people could not and would not ever do!! You need to show people that you do not need to be a pro-athlete to push yourself to your limits. This has nothing to do with your physical ability, purely mental. Finish this and you will be able to kick the shit out of anything and anyone. You better fucking finish this, or I will bug you for the rest of your life. I will call you all hours of the night and knock on your door interrupt all your presentations. I will haunt you forever and I mean it YOU BETTER FINISH!!!!

"It's not funny, I fucking mean it!! I'm not as nice as you think I am. I am watching you. You leave early and I'll have you arrested at the airport. I still

have connections. Prison is way worse than walking twelve hours a day. You can do this!!!! Keep me posted."

Needless to say, I got a good night's sleep, tied on my boots and headed out the next day for another twenty-eight kilometers.

If it's beyond your control, change your perception, creatively cope or quit complaining. If it's within your control and exhausting you, then change it.

When I look at how we do our work and live today, I see a huge population of people who are living further away from their jobs, making the commute just to *get to* work stressful. In bigger cities, we will spend on average an hour and a half a day commuting. Now, when you add that to your average working day of eight hours (depending on how stressful that is), it starts to compound and these two environments either becomes energizing or exhausting. For most of us, our environment is contributing to our chaos.

If you're a parent, add in the taxi service you provide to various activities and events and before you know it, you are now living in an environment of Busyness. So here's the deal: you can choose to change how you see it, literally change where and how you do your work or find ways to help the commute become less stressful for you. But this is your reality. You now get to decide what you're going to do about it. Complaining about it is like spinning your wheels in snow: you probably will find someone to commiserate with you, but you really should have bought snow tires in the first place. If you really want to try something new today, write the words "No is an option" on a sticky note and put it on your computer. Give it a try.

We can strike a balance between *"you better fucking finish this,"* as Leah so nicely put it, and creatively finding ways to decrease the exhaustion that we feel our environments are contributing to. And if we choose not to take the initiative to find ways to calmly cope or initiate change, then we at least need to stop complaining. We've created the lives we live.

CHAPTER 13

Disconnect to Re-Engage and Notice What You Notice

Breaking Busy: If your electronic device dictates your
day, it's time to *power down.*

OK people, I've said it in my last book *Shift...or Get Off the Pot* and it bears mentioning again: **PUT DOWN THE CELL PHONE**, smart phone, stupid phone, iPad or whatever you call the gadget that has become the object of your infinite affection and attention! Get your heads out of your crotches and **LOOK UP!**

Are you hooked on Electronics?

Fact: IPSOS Poll Shows across North America:

- 92% of Knowledge Workers (folks who use a computer at work) read, send, make or take work-related communications in *non-work* situations

- 73% have keep their communication devices on over the weekend

- 45% still tune into the office while on vacation

- More than half of the working population (55%) communicate about work in social situations, while spending time with their families, over dinner or on dates and about 20% have cut a date short to take a work call or respond to a work message.

- 6% of the population says that they always ignore the request to turn off phones while in meetings, church, plays and movie theatres.

A man was shot in a movie theatre by an upset viewer when he did not leave his phone alone.

Why do we keep up with this obsession behavior? Has our environment and culture truly dictated that we do so or has our doing so created our culture? What's the payoff to our addiction? Those are the big questions, let alone all the effects of these habits that we continue to condone.

I spent the good part of thirty-two days disconnected from the electronic world with nothing to check for or notice, except the organic elements of my physical, mental, emotional and spiritual body and the environment that I found myself in. When we disconnect, it sure doesn't take long to realize how over-connected we have become. It's in the twitching of your hand that needs to press a button every few minutes, the vibrating on your hip that gives you a burst of excitement, the little voice in your head (ego) that wants to check your messages or that internal crying for that "I'm needed" emotional boost of self-importance.

Have we really whittled down our ability to connect face-to-face with people and replaced it with the "skill" of conversing via our current version of *virtually crafted relationships*?

I took the test while walking the Camino. Is it time for yours? And where will you take it?

Do you need a Disconnected Detox?

1. If you have checked for messages in the past ten minutes, then you need to detox.

2. If you have ever scrolled emails over the dinner table, then you need to detox.

3. If you check messages and emails while on vacation, right after making love to your partner or while the kids opened their Christmas or birthday gifts, then you need to detox.

4. If you have to peak at the electronic screen during your weekly visit

to Church, the Synagogue, Mosque or your in-laws, then you need to detox.

5. Plain and simple: if you own and electronic gadget of any sort, then you need to detox.

What's the Upside?

On a single day without being glued to your device, you might be pleasantly surprised by just how many hours there actually are in a day.

There is a video currently trending on YouTube called "Look Up." It's an honest look at how disconnected we have all become. We don't even know what we are missing as the world passes us by while we stare at our phones. We have built non-real relationships with friends who are not really our friends. We have so many connections, but no real intimate moments.

My seventeen-year-old daughter, Josee, can name twenty of her friends who have been broken up with over text in this past year and emoticons are the only way we know how to add texture to our conversations.

Seriously, LOOK UP! Your next best friend might be standing in front of you.

Being engaged in something, whether it's your work, your relationships or yourself means having a current conscious awareness of more than just the electronic beckoning that you've surrounded yourself with at any given time. It means giving a damn about what you are doing and consciously making decisions to give it your all. Here's to shifting towards Re-Engagement. **LOOK UP from your phone**.

CHAPTER 14

An Attempt to Kind-a Disconnect and Sort-a Re-Engage

Breaking Busy: Figure out what you really truly need to be happy, and dedicate yourself to it.

On the Camino de Santiago in 2014, ninety-eight percent of all bars, cafés, Albergues and hotels have WiFi. There is a cell service everywhere. What really helped me in my attempt to disconnect was that making calls or using 3G for any data was way out of my budget; so I would only connect with my life back home in the evenings for an hour. Many places only had sporadic WiFi, which forced me to do other things, such as sleep. The only phone calls I made were to my parents in Alberta, Canada, as my Dad has never used a computer and my mom likes me to call. Once a week on Fridays, when I would finish my grueling daily walk, I would order a cold beer and call home.

My Dad told me that he had gone down to the local Motor Association and bought a map of Spain. He and Mom have never traveled outside of North America. He'd ask my Mom where I was and would follow me on his map with a ruler. (A concept that I told him that his grandchildren could never fathom.) I thought the gesture was very sweet and was one of the highlights of my entire trip. Knowing that they were checking out my progress every day made me feel just a little less alone; even more so than any Facebook post someone could have made or the endless line of emails sitting in my inbox. At fifty-three years of age, I felt like I was twelve and my parents were cheering me on.

From the standpoint of "productivity," we all need to disconnect simply to *get stuff done*. Our Busyness is keeping us from making time for being deeply inspired or taking the time to follow someone across a map, so to speak.

I am seriously not sure how my teenage daughters get their homework done and pull off the marks they do because as they read, write and create, they are constantly writing, reading and responding to texts, snap chats, etc. It truly takes discipline (or as my coach calls it, "Bubble Time") to get actual work done.

Isabelle Mercier has coached me to carve out time to be creative and productive. She'd tell me to ensure that all email notifications are off - the phone is off - and that I have "however you define a 'Rockstar'" start to the day. My start includes getting the kids off to school, making breakfasts and lunches, taking my two dogs for some exercise, coming back home for a shower, hair and makeup and landing myself in the office. There I check mail, clear paper on desk and turn everything off. "Bubble Time."

What's your formula? The best part is that you can write your own! And truthfully, you HAVE TO. If you don't have one, then one year from now, we will be having the same conversation about how you never have time to get to the stuff you really want to.

Make sure that your formula includes checking in with your daily and weekly cheerleaders - the people who cheer you on from the sidelines. If your system has the right ingredients, then your energy and flow will naturally evolve.

How you do anything is pretty much how you do everything.

Ideas for Designing Your Perfectly Productive Day:

Live like a Rockstar. Figure out what combination of practices makes you feel like a Rockstar before you get to work. This can include exercise, reading, meditation, walking your dog, showering, dressing in a Rockstar wardrobe, etc.

Use the 80/20 rule. Focus your time on the 20% of your efforts that produce 80% of your results. You already instinctively know what these are.

Take more frequent shorter breaks. It is critical that you get out of your chair at least once an hour. The "sitting crisis" is non-negotiable.

Be mighty in the morning. Plan and attack your toughest project or to-do before lunch. This is when your energy and focus is at its peak. (Set "Bubble Time" here with zero interruptions.)

Improve your email routine. Only check your email once an hour, just after you have sat down from your hourly stretch break. Turn off the noise on all devices so that you don't know messages and emails have come in until you physically check.

Stop multi tasking. No, you are *not* effective at multi tasking.

Be honest with yourself. Writing emails, excessively organizing, and setting and attending meetings are sometimes facades for actually doing real work.

Perform a weekly cleanup. Set a designated hour, once a week, to clean up your inboxes.

It's YOUR DAY; make it work for you.

CHAPTER 15

Rest Up and Clear the Chatter

Every day was another day to be in my own head,
no clutter, just thought…
—Linda Edgecombe

Breaking Busy: If your mind is overwhelmed, make
some room for quiet, inside and out.

In Spain, what I found mentally challenging was how quiet it was. I had no idea how few pilgrims would be out there at that time of year. I went from early March to mid April and it as shocking to me how few people I actually saw. Most small towns seemed like ghost towns and lord help me if I hit a town during Siesta "2-6pm: Closed."

A few weeks in, my body wasn't as sore. So what else did I do? *Think, think, think*, about anything and everything. I cried, got mad, got sad and spent plenty of time bored or just looking at the ground thinking, "I hope that tonight's hostel will be comfortable." It may have been quiet all around me, but it surely wasn't quiet in my head.

The only other time in my life that I had to really dig deep mentally was when I visited Nepal with my husband, Kevin. We went to see the girls we had been fundraising for and rescued from child-bonded labor for several years through IWEN. I knew going in that I was going to be challenged with poverty and my big fear of not being comfortable. What can I say, I like a nice thread count, I value clean bathrooms and the thought of bedbugs, well, kind of bugs me.

Poverty is something that permeates all of our senses to the point that it becomes overwhelming. But I have to say that whenever I hear a song that I listened to while I was in Nepal, I am back there instantly. As a trip, it affected me more than any other to date in my life.

So when I over-planned my trip to the Camino, I tried to prepare myself by reading everything I could. As it turned out, without a doubt, the Camino was nowhere near the same place as Nepal. While it had mental strains of its own, there was no saturation of poverty weighing so heavily on the mind.

Although they both affected me in different ways, it embarrasses me to say that neither the Camino or the trip to Nepal made me tougher, at least not yet. My *suck it up buttercup* moment didn't really happen. Maybe my adventure is meant to come in some other form. Maybe its time to shop for a motor home or maybe, I just need to slow things down and take a more intrinsically-focused adventure...

I guess I am not the *total adventurer* that I had hoped I would be; but either way, I look forward to whatever comes next.

Over the years, I have often asked what would you do if you were given the gift of a few bonus hours in the day. Most recently, I asked my readers what they would do, given an extra hour? Hands down, by a landslide, their answer was SLEEP.

The "Busy Life" we've created is mentally draining us. It's taking up all space of our lives and overwhelming our minds. So instead of purposely deciding what to carve out of our lives to create some space, we would rather shut down and make it go away. We'd rather sleep.

According to the National Center for Sleep Disorders Research at the National Institutes of Health, about thirty to forty percent of adults say that they have some symptoms of insomnia. The definition of insomnia is "the inability to fall or remain asleep." I can speak from the experience, living with a very busy husband who has been suffering from insomnia for years. (I'm happy to say that he has recently begun taking his sleep issues seriously and has sought out some help.)

We strain our minds to think through our Busyness. We don't sleep and then, we're too darn tired for our minds to even work properly, so we strain them some more trying. You can't function without enough sleep.

The one blessing of taking a long walk across Spain was realizing the benefit of letting my brain go. I worked out whatever I needed to think through (and really questioned what was necessary to think about) and left everything that had been running through my mind scattered along the trail.

At home, I walk about one hour every morning with my dogs. It's the place and time where I get to clear my head and find most of my creative ideas. So if nothing else, get busy walking. Not away from your mind, but with it - carving out that space of quiet.

CHAPTER 16

Our Decisions Aren't Made in a Vacuum

Breaking Busy: Busyness leads to hovering, and hovering doesn't really lead anywhere.

I recently listened to Canadian Astronaut Admiral Chris Hatfield speak at an event where he suggested that decision-making is a diminishing skill. He explained that we need to continuously practice decision-making so when it comes to making big choices, we've already made some bad ones. What we need to do is learn how to make big decisions and then, practice the heck out of doing so. More importantly, we can allow our teams and families to make choices on their own and deal with the consequences of their decisions.

When I wrote *Shift...or Get Off the Pot*, the basic underlying message was to *make a decision already!* In spite of what we've heard for ages, we actually tend to not flee *or* fight; we just freeze. I call this *the world that hovers*. The great majority of us hover and I believe we do so for a few reasons. For most of us, *here* is not bad at all. We are pretty *OK* with where we are - not ecstatic, not disgusted, just *OK*. And for a few of us, even if *here* is hell, it's the hell we know; so we stay, thinking the hell we know is better than the fear of not knowing what's *out there* beyond our current circumstances.

How does our choice to hover play out in our day-to-day lives?

When most of us try and make decisions, we mainly way the pros and cons of the situation. For instance, you're questioning whether to take a new job. You write out the pros and cons of taking the job and the pros and cons of not taking the job. The key is to then do a gut check. What is your gut or intuition telling you? Logic + feeling usually equals good decision-making. It seems really successful people make more good decisions than bad…or do they?

George Pitagorsky in *Project Times* says, "There are three primary ways to make a decision in a group: by authority, by majority and by consensus. Compromise, conflict avoidance and assertiveness, dialog, debate and facilitation are techniques used in the decision-making process. The art of decision-making calls for the practical application of these in an approach that depends on the needs of the situation." There is no absolute one best way. All of the above are skills that take practice, so start practicing.

When pressed, the majority of people will either make a spontaneous decision, which leads to what is known as "buyer's remorse," or we get overwhelmed, shut down and make no decisions at all.

Are any of these hitting a nerve yet? In Section 3 of this book, I am going to give you the fast track to a life of decision-making that will no longer be stressful. It's not an easy transition, but if you really want off the "Busy Treadmill," this one tactic is key.

Deciding to do the Camino was easy. I was so inspired and knew instantly that I had to go. It was a decision driven by what I knew I had to do for myself. I didn't over-think the details. All I knew from what I had researched was that I didn't want to go in the summer because it would be far too hot and busy; so I thought either spring or fall. The rest of the decisions fell into place from there.

The instant gut-driven decision to go quickly became a long-term decision because its execution required at least four to five weeks of dedicated time. My other deciding factor in going early in the season was that my daughter Josee plays girls' fastball and not even a life-changing Camino walk could keep me from my LOVE of ball! I love it so much that I chose to leave mid March and return Mid April, just in time for ball season to begin. That put me in Spain at precisely the rainiest time of year.

My decision-making had set me up for a soggy long-term haul in the (dis)comfort of my own company. Seeking out that "finding myself moment," I insisted on going by myself. It wasn't an easy decision... I had been having overwhelming thoughts about needing to create some new stories in my life and felt that I hadn't in a long time. Quite frankly, going alone scared the shit out of me, but I did it. Maybe I'm a Martyr just for making that decision because it really did seem like a good idea at the time.

Hovering might have been an easier way to trespass over eight-hundred kilometers, though it sure wouldn't have yielded the same awareness and lasting lessons as taking full action and deciding not only to walk The Camino, but to also face every challenge that came my way along those thirty-two demanding days. I can honestly say that if I knew what the experience was going to be like, I probably wouldn't have gone. I would have just stayed home, hovered and watched *The Way* a few more dozen times. So I paid my money and got what I got. That's how life is dished out, now isn't it?

What is being Busy keeping you from truly doing? What realizations and actions are you holding back on, sitting in "hover lane"?

CHAPTER 17

The Silent Company of Loneliness

Breaking Busy: If you've forgotten who you truly are,
then it's time to put the brakes on busy.

When I was in my twenties, the most comfortable I felt in my own skin was when I was traveling. It may have been because I didn't have to act like anyone but *me*. Now that I'm in my fifties, I'm not truly sure who that person is. Once I learned how to cope with the physical, environment and mental strains of my journey, I was hoping that I might find *her*.

In this "Busy Culture" we've created, we have left very little time to feel. Each day plays out like a racquetball game with us just responding to where the ball is hit. We don't actually have to feel anything; we just react. And every once and a while, when we do slow down long enough to allow some emotions to stir, we usually quickly distract ourselves from the discomfort of feeling. We turn on the TV, eat food and drink alcohol, use humor, do housework or just work. This is not a judgment - it's human behavior. It's just our survival defense mechanism kicking in.

Personally, Kevin and I have had a very stressful past couple of years with business and financial pressures, physical injuries, etc. As we sat watching this past winter's Olympics and watched one Canadian athlete's parents talk about their daughter's gold medal performance, we were both in tears. I chalked it up to it being touching and a feeling we could relate to as parents; but on a deeper level, Kevin and I needed to have a good cry and that interview allowed us to open the floodgates.

The great thing about physical pain is that it distracts from thinking about and facing deeper pains. On the Camino, those pains included loneliness, missing my girls, wondering what is needed to keep my twenty-nine year relationship with my husband alive and questioning if I really wanted to keep my speaking business going. I've been speaking professionally for over twenty-four years. I've seen more than my share of airports and airplanes and with all my accomplishments, I somehow still don't truly believe that I'm enough. How is that?

There was also the pain I caused myself. Self-loathing had become my all-too-frequent guest. As I trudged along, kilometer after kilometer, I wondered why I don't really try and make my speaking career fly higher than I have or why I couldn't just be a skinny broad instead of a chubby humorist. So long as that physical pain was ringing through my every joint and muscle, it was all I had to think about. Well, that and how many dudes I would be sleeping with the coming night.

About five days into the Camino walk, I noticed how I sounded to myself, in my own head, was no different than I did when I am at home. It literally took me until the last week of the journey to notice that I was no longer beating myself up. My self-judgments had simply *stopped*.

We're working ever harder in our "Busy Culture" and we're beating ourselves up for doing it. Perhaps because we no longer know how to just be with ourselves, without judgment, criticism or thoughts of what we *should* be doing, rather than spending time alone. So what do we do about it?

Getting outdoors is critical to being connected to ourselves. Find ways to be in nature that feel good for you to take care of your physical and mental wellbeing. Let nature's beauty and silence help you to find the connection to yourself.

What is the best place for you to hear your own voice? To feel your true emotions?

When we truly connect with ourselves, in a place of peace and silence, we learn to recognize the messages that our body and mind are trying to relay to us. That voice will tell you what you need to do to feel better and achieve a better quality of everyday life. It's an act more simple than most of what we take on in our busy lives. And when you start to simplify your life, you will find and create space to **feel more**.

When the third week on the Camino rolled around, I found myself crying at least once a day for almost any reason. My girls missed me and I missed them, my mom was not feeling great, I didn't feel a part of the "Camino club," my body wasn't looking any different and I was utterly exhausted. I mean, seriously, how many kilometers a day does a girl have to walk to lose a pound?

I hadn't really had what I would call a good connection with anyone in almost fifteen days. I was painfully lonely.

Why did I insist on doing this stupid trip alone? I didn't have anyone to commiserate with at the end of each day to make the experience more of a community one, but it sure was quiet.

What I realize that I gained in the quiet was the ability to take *a lot* of time to think and feel. Now, a few months after my return home, I am just coming into the awareness of how I hold space where my emotions can just *be*.

In the first few weeks of coming home, I had no filter to help me block out negative feelings and discussions. I actually felt low-level physical pain when someone talked about something that was negative going on in the world. As strange as it may sound, I couldn't physically handle hearing bad stories or details in the news. Several weeks later, I didn't build a brick wall back around myself, but just allowed myself to feel and recognize where I am. It's so easy to feel overwhelmed when we're immersed in the Busy Life, and coming out of that and allowing ourselves to feel our emotions in a whole new way (and let them go) takes time.

The added benefit of connecting with ourselves, simplifying and feeling, is that it naturally leads us to filter the eternal events, people and circumstances in our lives. You start to eliminate the things that waste your time and energy or meaningless to you. You learn how to shield yourself from negativity and you begin to accept **only the best**.

We need to start to do more things that promote wellbeing and spend more time with people who make us happy. We need to start doing all the things that we don't make time for when we're Busy. This is what life is truly about, but you have to take action to get there. If you just think, plan and don't act, then nothing changes in your life and your wellbeing and quality of everyday life doesn't get any better.

Even if it's a little lonely at first, give yourself a little quiet time. You might just find yourself there.

CHAPTER 18

Exposing the Truths of Vulnerability

Breaking Busy: If you haven't let yourself feel uncomfortable in a while, do so.

The only thing that is truly ours on the planet is our stories and the only reason we are on the planet is to connect to other people. Every one of us is literally in "the people business." In spite of what you may think, you are *not* in the accounting business or healthcare profession. You are not a homebuilder, real estate agent or any other titled role. You are in the helping-people-create-the-best-life-they-can-possibly-create business. So with that said, I will repeat: **the only reason we are on the planet is to connect with other people**. And the only way we connect to other people is through our stories.

Life isn't about the details of the work you do. There is not one person in the past twenty-four years that I have been speaking and writing who has ever quoted the twelve steps to reducing stress that I have taught them, but they can repeat any personal story I've told them. So if connection happens with stories, then you need to know that the only way we truly connect is when we are vulnerable. We need to show our underbelly. You don't have to put it ALL on your sleeve, but opening up and connecting is and can be your game changer. People don't relate to your graphs and stats; they relate to you being a parent, a friend, a traveler, a pet owner or a teacher. You capture them by being real about your screw-ups and your wins.

Think of it this way: being vulnerable just means your stories are just data with a soul. They are what you have to share without fear of what anyone thinks about them. We've lost this lovin' feeling on the way to our being Busy.

For the past few years, Brené Brown has had one of the most poignant, highest viewed TED Talks on the topic of Vulnerability. She tells us that *in order live your life "whole heartedly," you have to have the courage to be flawed.* And we all need to know this one fact: there is not one of us on the planet who has it together. No one does. So save yourself some energy and stop trying to look like the way you do.

Authentic people fully embrace vulnerability. They believe what made them vulnerable is what made them beautiful. They say I love you first.

I knew before I left for the Camino that I like to try to control any situation that might make me uncomfortable. Discomfort for me means actually becoming physically uncomfortable. I started getting pickier as to where I would stay at night, which only further compounded my awful feelings of loneliness. The comfortable Albergue was the quiet one, far removed from other people. I'd sit alone in that hostel room and beat myself up because I wasn't as adventurous as I thought I should be.

We need to stop controlling and predicting every turn. We are depriving ourselves of opportunities to grow and to allow unexpected possibility to appear.

When there is a lack of vulnerability, we find shame. Fear and shutdown follows. Most of us don't want to feel afraid or shameful, so we do our best not to feel anything at all. And with enough practice, we can get pretty good at it. So indifference sets in, but then it's tough to come back to a place of actually allowing ourselves to *feel*.

Vulnerability is the birthplace of love, kindness, joy, creativity and belonging - a literal opening of our hearts. I experienced it first-hand when I dropped my ego's fear and pride surrounding my own finances. I got honest, reached out for help and became vulnerable; and it feels, to this day, like a brick wall has been taken off of my shoulders. It wasn't much different than peeling back those layers and trekking along the Camino.

For years, I prided myself and called myself an *Alberta-born Broad*, tough and not too emotional - a *get-er-done* kind of lady. I am also not a person who easily walks into being tender, kind and loving. And to be able to say *sorry*, well, that was mighty challenging. I saw the need to apologize as being weak and that kind of vulnerability scared the crap out of me.

Brené says that *most of us numb vulnerability - having to ask for help, initiating for sex, apologizing, looking at good friends in the eyes with love and compassion.* We are the most obese, in-debt, co-dependent group of adults ever! So we eat, drink and laugh away the hard feelings. When we numb the hard stuff, we numb happiness.

Start to just wonder. Say things like *why, that's interesting, I wonder why I feel that way.* Don't just respond to things. Be curious. Start to heighten your senses, enjoy views, foods, laughs and sex longer. Stop perfecting your kids and for God's sake, stop living vicariously through them. They need a parent to show them how to open their hearts. Let yourself be deeply seen by everyone close to you.

Say that you are worthy of love and belonging every day. Love with your whole heart. Practice gratitude and joy. And most importantly, **Believe You are Enough!!!**

Here's to a more vulnerable day!

CHAPTER 19

Nothing But Time: An Unexpected Silent Retreat

Breaking Busy: You're already enough. You don't need
to do more to prove it.

For those of you who know me as Linda Edgecombe, the social and animated speaker, you know that me being on a "Silent Retreat" seems almost amusing. However, according to the work and research of Dr. Brian Little, I am what you call an *Ambi-vert* - not an introvert and not an extrovert, just somewhere in the middle. Oh, I can hear the calls of "Bull shit!" coming in loud and clear. You know me as an extrovert, but the truth is that while I'm a great outgoing performer, I also need retreat time, alone.

When I booked myself on this walking holiday, I had *no idea* that it would end up being a silent retreat. That social extroverted side of me thought that I would be meeting people from all over the world. Being as exciting a person as I am, I had convinced myself that I would have to ask people to *not* walk with me so that I could spend some a little time "thinking." Needless to say, I never had to ask anyone to let me walk alone because there was NO one to ask anything to. I ended up with way more "thinking time" than I bargained for. What is so surprising to me is that I thought I knew *how* to be alone.

My daily life consists of working by myself, travelling for work by myself, speaking on stage and heading back to my hotel by myself. I even eat in restaurants all the time by myself. I quickly discovered that *being by myself* and *feeling alone* were two *very* different things. I had never felt the pain of loneliness like I did on the Camino. It actually hurt in my body.

Feeling that pain, I did what I normally do: I internalized the experience as if there was something wrong with me. *I'm not fast enough, dedicated enough, skinny enough or friendly enough.* You get the picture.

On rare occasions, I would spot another pilgrim. If they spoke any English, I chatted them up to the point of over-communicating, attempting to break from feeling so alone. And then funny enough, they carried on their way and I never saw them again. This was also a new experience for me - building relationships that went no further than a brief exchange.

In total, over my thirty-two day walk across Spain's Camino de Santiago de Compestella, I had six days of walking where I had another human being to talk to and twenty-six days of endless solitude; just me and God and eventually, a little rock and roll.

The truth is, I didn't much like myself before I left for this trip. So why did I think that I would do a *180* and end up liking myself when I was there?

One week prior to leaving, I had gone to see the documentary movie *Walking the Camino – Six ways to Santiago.* One of the pilgrims featured in the movie said, "You won't find God on the Camino, you have to bring him with you." Maybe it was my cue to say that if I don't like me at home, how's Spain going to make that change? The old saying that you follow yourself wherever you go had never been more true. Every self-depreciating thought in my head and aching pain in my body were my constant companions; and by day seventeen, their weight became a bit too much to carry.

I decided to start forgiving myself for any and all my perceived mess-ups. I'd pick up a rock, jog my memory and remember something I had done, said or thought about that wasn't me being at my best. I'd rub those memories into the rock and then I'd find a place to put it somewhere on the trail. Sometimes I left them on a cross, other times on a monument; I even placed them in the middle of the fields. And truthfully, I started to feel lighter.

I was feeling better about my past choices and decisions, not as if they mattered any less, but as though they were no longer my burdens to carry. With that weight lifted off my shoulders (in addition to shedding some of the unnecessary items from my overly-packed pack, I was beginning to see myself a little clearer. Oh, the sweet irony: no sooner did I come to such a revelation did the trail become a very flat and very visible straight path. It was as if I was walking across Saskatchewan, with small bars/cafés every five kilometer. Five hundred and twenty-five kilometers, thirty, thirty-five...

While it was still unbelievably easy to get caught up in my thoughts, I found myself in a bit of a walking mediation. I could clearly see my direction and somehow felt as though I had a lot of open space to breathe.

It was time to change the story of my life. I have been on the procrastination fence (hover lane, if you will) for almost ten years now with small bursts of determination, discipline and energy. The major underlying tone for me has been a massive wave of self-loathing and I hated myself for hating myself. I am highly aware of what I have going for me and have such a hard time believing it. That is what I really noticed while I was on my pilgrimage across Spain.

Now don't worry, I did have my "revolutionary realization" during my last week on this walk. It also became very clear that unless we find a silent space and take a few things off our busy plates, we just won't have the ability to be open for any kind of spiritual connection or develop a sense of faith (or whatever you believe in) in our lives. So, how will you start to make space?

Taking one hour on a Sunday to create it is not how it is supposed to happen. It may happen then, but I think you can have a spiritual moment on a Tuesday morning over coffee with your Grandma or with one of your students on a Thursday just before the school bus leaves. The intention is to create and hold space for this part of our lives to be experienced and cherished.

By the time I started walking the last hundred kilometers, I never once had the self-loathing voice in my head. I remember thinking that it simply felt great to feel great. Perhaps my "divine intervention" on this trip was to figure out that I had to actually like myself to feel as though I was "enough." When I did so, all of a sudden, people started showing up wanting to talk to me. Go figure…

Look in the mirror and say, "You are enough". Repeat it several times daily. Say it until *you* believe it. You may have forgotten it while busily hovering through life, but trust me, it's true.

CHAPTER 20

The Elusive Search for Happiness

Breaking Busy: If you don't like the shape of your life,
slice out some happiness.

By the last week of my trek, I had found my stride. I was easily walking twenty-seven to thirty-five kilometers a day. Even the rain didn't bother me as much.

There is this rule on the Camino: if you walk and obtain proof that you have completed the last one-hundred kilometers, you will get your *Compestella* - your fast track to heaven, as I understand it.

Only having to complete the final hundred kilometers to get a fast track to heaven seems somewhat unfair for those of us who have already put in seven hundred kilometers, but it's the rule. Because of the honor that it holds, the last hundred kilometers are much busier than the first seven hundred. Not only was I finally seeing people on a daily basis, but I also had found a gear in my legs and easily walked by many of them (even on the up-hills) as my competitive side started coming out. My spirit and energy simply felt lighter, perhaps because I could see and feel the finish line. I enjoyed chatting with strangers and felt a glow of energy radiating from my face. Never once was there the self-loathing voice in my head putting me down. It just simply wasn't there. Perhaps I had left it several hundred kilometers back in a rock, somewhere in a deep lush field.

My mom posted on my Facebook page that she wasn't surprised at my pace near the end of the trek because I used to skip to school when I was young. I think I need to start skipping again. Maybe we *all* just need to start skipping again with the lightness of not being weighed down by everything we've done or said in the days that are now so very far in the past.

As it turned out, peeling off the layers on the Camino and in life, isn't simply about taking off warmer layers when the rain and winds clear and we find our stride. It's about freeing ourselves of all the stuff we no longer need to carry so that we can let our true selves joyfully smile, shine and skip through every day of life. Just like we talked about in Section 1, happy people don't worry about what other people think.

What I know is that everyone has his or her own recipe for happiness. I also know that most people haven't even thought about what their ingredients are. Ironically, we keep going after it every day, but we don't know what creates the stars, so we trek along hoping they will line up.

What makes you say *Ahhh* or calls you to say *Yum*? What situations, big or small, simply make you smile? Where do you rest your soul when you are stressed?

Choose a Slice of the Planet and become Happier. That's the ingredient we've lost when our recipe has been for Busyness alone.

If you are reading this book because your life has become a crazy routine of work, home, family, renovations, fundraising etc, then I am going to make an assumption that you are living a pretty good life. The quality of your days may need some tweaking, but you are not wanting for much, except more time perhaps. When we get to this stage, we realize something is missing and what's missing is usually time to "give back."

I call this *Choosing a Slice of the Planet* because when we are privileged, what comes along with that privilege is responsibility. You can choose a *slice* that is right outside your door, in your community or on the other side of the planet. The important thing is that you choose. When we do something kind for someone else, what happens is physical - your Vegas nerve fires off a shot of endorphins into your system, giving your that Hallmark card feeling of warmth and happiness.

The two researchers - Elizabeth Dunn, a UBC psychology professor, and Michael Norton, a marketing professor at Harvard Business School - analyzed data from Canada, India, South Africa and one-hundred and thirty-six other countries and have compiled the information in a new book called *Happy Money: The Science of Smarter Spending.*

What they discovered was that people around the world, both rich and poor, experience emotional rewards when using their money to benefit others. The evidence was so compelling that the authors believe that they may have found a psychologically universal human trait.

What's even better is that you can donate your time, your skills or your money to get this great feeling. This is an important part of "the Camino" you are currently walking on.

To help speed up those good feelings, I have summarized **5 Quick Tips to Becoming Happier**, with the disclaimer that it seems ironic to say so when, in so many cases, we have lots to be happy for. We have the freedom, challenges, experiences and opportunities to live a life filled with success, adventure, outstanding memories and chances to do things that are amazing. Nonetheless, here they are:

Tip 1: Smile. Sounds obvious, but honestly when I walk down the street, there are more sullen faces than smiles. Just take some time in the next few days to become aware of those around you and whether they are smiling. Be aware of whether *you* are smiling. It takes some effort if you don't smile naturally, but it is well worth it. Smiling can trick the body into helping you change your mood.

Tip 2: Pull out Pictures of Happy Times. Now this may mean digging deep into the back of the closet or searching your computer, but again, it is well worth the time. Check out all the fun you have had and all the experiences you've been a part of. Reflect on what happened at the exact moment the picture was taken

Tip 3: Get Moving. These tips can't be "Linda Edgecombe tips" unless it includes the importance of get moving. Now, many of you might be thinking, how does moving help your happiness? Well, when you get moving, you get out of your head and stop thinking about the challenges that are making you unhappy. Through movement, you release endorphins, natural hormones that flood the body with a feel-good energy - a natural high! You release stress through physical exertion and regulated breathing so that you can let go of the day's challenges and feel relaxed and refreshed. Try something you love to do like dancing, hiking, yoga, golf or anything that you enjoy.

Tip 4: Find a Happiness Friend. So, that sounds a little silly, but I've said it before: surround yourself with people who are happy, positive and see the bright side of life. When you spend time with happy people, they start to rub off on you. The energy and enthusiasm is contagious if you let it be.

Tip 5: Practice Being Happy. No matter what, it takes awareness and effort to be happy. We are challenged everyday with the negative - from the articles that question how happy you are to people you work with or find yourself in the company of who seem to see things from a unhappy perspective.

Happiness is a state of mind! Your mind is flexible and open to change. It just needs a little help. Take it for a walk on the happy side. (And that walk doesn't necessarily have to be eight-hundred kilometres long.)

CHAPTER 21

Even if You Don't Walk The Camino, You Still Walk A Camino

Breaking Busy: **You** decide when you "Break Busy" and Realize Happiness.

As we all know, there are really no directional maps of life telling us where we should go. We have our parents to guide us when we're young and our communities and institutions to set some moral boundaries, but for the most part, life is a figure-it-out-as-you-go experience. And with a solid foundation, most of us create a life that we are comfortable with.

When walking the Camino, there are several guidebooks to choose from to give you an idea of the terrain and the options of where to sleep and tidbits on history, but you mainly just look for way markers - signs that indicate you are going in the right direction.

What are your "way markers" in life?

Most of the markers on the Camino were identifiable yellow arrows and seashells; though every once and a while, I would come to a crossroad and not see a marker. If I allowed myself a moment and looked again (and sometimes twice), I would always find my sign. Sometimes we need to see a situation with new eyes or a new perspective; and when we do, the answer is usually right there in front of us.

Life's not always easy; we know that. We *will* get lost and that's OK.

On a few and far between instances, I got lost on the Camino; and when it happened, I wasn't afraid to ask for or accept direction. There was the farmer on his tracker, plowing his spring fields, who honked his horn until I looked up and he was able to point me back on track and then, there was the instance of knowing that I was lost in the city of León and was willing to ask for help.

On most days, I had no idea where I would end up. It's a lifestyle that parallels everyday life. You have a plan. Sometimes you get to the end of it and sometimes, you have to pick up a sick kid from school, spend two hours looking for your dog who went on his own trek around town or shift direction when your boss throws in a last minute emergency meeting. Remember my niece's five-year-old plan for her life and how differently reality played out? Our parents generation, nor we as children, would never have predicted how Busy our generation would become.

The 1960's term "Go with the flow" was in relation to pushing back against ridged military thinking and creating a more flexible frame of being. As I said at the very beginning of this section of the book, "being in control is highly overrated." If we allow ourselves a little give, it's amazing how far we'll get.

So how does my walking trek relate to the rest of the planet who may never journey the Camino? Think about it this way: most of us have goals, jobs, families, mortgages and everyday circumstances to live with. Sometimes life gets very challenging and we wind up with body pain from the stress we endure. We are handed projects that make us stretch mentally. Some of us have jobs we dread going to. Relationships can fall apart or just hit speed bumps or we can go days without anyone talking to us. On occasion, a few times every year, we can also have one of those "it doesn't get any better than this moments."

Before leaving for my adventure, I had heard several times that "The Camino provides whatever you need." Upon reflection, I guess I needed to be uncomfortable, lonely, occasionally lost and stubborn enough to stick it out in order to find my fitness again and scratch out a new sense of self. In our everyday lives, sometimes we face an entire grueling Camino in one day. Some of us have been walking through the first couple of weeks for years, never getting past the physical strain to the 'enlightened' stretch. The truth is that it is **each of us** who gets to decide how long we take to reach the point where we come alive with that true sense of self and deep-rooted happiness. We get to decide how much time we spend hovering, trekking or breaking from our busyness to find ourselves. We get to decide when we cut ourselves a little slack.

If your life feels out of control, bursting at all edges, there's a reason. We all get our personal little reminders to jump off the Busy treadmill: headaches, the inability to sleep, short fuses, exhaustion, etc. If we don't pay attention to the signs, we get lost…and the signs might just get bigger and strike again. We then gain weight, lose relationships, face illness, come into financial stress, have career upheaval, etc. You just need to recognize your signs and adjust your recipe for happiness accordingly.

When we step back, it's not hard to see what our Busy Culture is doing to us. Take the time to realize what is working and what isn't and be prepared to make some small shifts to create what it is you **really want**… not just in your mind or in the grumbling of your stomach, but with every ounce of who you are. That is what we'll cover in the last section of this book. It's time!

SECTION 3:

Finding Peace in the Chaos

CHAPTER 22

What Do You REALLY Want?

Breaking Busy: Think less. Fearlessly leap more.

When I first started asking my readers the question "What do you REALLY want?", the most common answer would begin with a lot of *Umm*s and *Ahh*s followed by, "I don't know...I just don't know."

The truth is, I believe you do know. What we don't want to do is admit that we know because if we admit that we know, then we may have to do something about it. So what do we do? We sit neck-deep in the dilemma of wanting to carry on with our everyday lives, honoring that perceived fear-based need to not change anything, while hearing and begin tending to the slow burn of desires and dreams that is gnawing at our souls and spirits.

Note: Thinking about making a change is usually more difficult than the change itself.

As we saw in Section 1, the pattern most of the planet has chosen is to be stuck in this "hover mode." Relating back to the *Busy Audit*, the top three reasons that keep us from making a change (doing what we really want) are:

1. Fear

2. Not having time

3. Over-thinking

We are choosing to stay right where we are because we think it's safe and for the most part, not all that bad. But then, comes that gnawing again. "Now what?" we ask ourselves. There's no denying that something is missing. It echoes through our gut and makes appearances in our dreams. And yet, our bottom line belief is that if we keep our lives in a constant state of busy or clutter-filled, we just won't have to really think about what we really want. Or will we?

Let's take a closer look at the number one reason that ruled people's responses as to why they avoid change and what we can do about **FEAR**.

There have been hundreds, if not thousands, of books written on how to overcome our fears. Heck, I've even read *Feel the Fear and Do it Anyway* by Dr. Susan Jeffers, while on route to speak at a weekend workshop on fear. Yes, I have done that and I'm not afraid of telling you so.

While books are wonderful and can spur change and growth, it's applying what we've learned, or are beginning to learn, to our everyday lives, which really drives home change. My biggest lesson on fear came from two experiences in my life. The first was on holiday with my husband Kevin when he took me to hike the Grand Canyon in Arizona. If you have never been, you simply have to put it on your "Been there, done that" list.

We arrived, and like most tourists, went and stood at the Canyon's edge and marveled at the vast, overwhelming beauty of it all. Instantly Kevin says, "We have to hike into the canyon!" So, we headed over to the information office to get trail maps and advice. We were told that most people hike to the river, camp over at Phantom Ranch and then, hike back out early the next day before it becomes too hot. It didn't take long for us to replay, "We're in!" The park ranger then informed us that you need a reservation to stay at Phantom Ranch, and the next opening was in six weeks time.

We thought about it for ten minutes and Kevin suggested that we hike down and out in one day, no sleep over. We got the necessary supplies: backpack, water, energy bars, more water, sunscreen and two matching hats (to ward off sunstroke and to help us look cool). We set the alarm for 4:15a.m. and were at the trailhead by 4:30a.m. The canyon was just starting to get light and the sun wasn't up yet. We could already tell it was going to be one of those Arizona days that start out warm and end like an oven on broil. (As a important side-note, I had not walked more than an hour in several years. This was long before my Camino trek. You'll see the importance of this statement shortly.)

It took us four hours on the South Kabob trail to get to the Colorado River. We sat down and soaked our already well-broiled feet before completing our eight-hour walk out of the canyon in one-hundred and ten degree Fahrenheit weather. Yes, four hours in and *eight* hours out.

Here is my point: Was it hard? Hell yes. I would have never done it if I had known what I needed to know. Writing this, I see the obvious trend between the Canyon hike and Camino trek... While I did have a base level of fitness, it was barely enough to save me the $3000 cost of having to have a helicopter come and pull me out of the Canyon. However, being willing to take the risk of diving into something new (if you can call planting ourselves in a bone-day, boiling hot Canyon "diving"), opened up new pathways for me. My hiking confidence received a huge boost after that experience. That summer, I hiked on several mountain hikes and my fear of not being able to do it wasn't ever once present. Those little trails no longer scared me after taking on the Canyon. Go figure.

The second example of having life teach me first-hand about the power of facing and overcoming fear came when I finally took some singing classes. It's true. I have always wanted to be a singer, but knew that I was missing that one key ingredient: talent. My girlfriends encouraged me to sign up for lessons and I quickly found out that you sound pretty good when you sing with someone who's good! I was given the opportunity to cut two songs on a CD at a Studio, which made me feel like I was in hog heaven. Once they took off the back tracks, yikes, it was a little hard to listen to. But wait for it...my big fear-smashing day came when my teacher told me that I was going to be in a singing recital in a local café. I had a panic attack on my way to the event, but still pulled myself up on stage and sang. It was pretty bad actually, but once I was done, I felt like

I had conquered the world and that energy flowed into other aspects of my life.

I had more jam in my step for weeks. I made more business deals after that than I had in months. And once again, it hit me: courage doesn't come to you *before* you do something, it comes *after you have walked through it* (or sung through it). So to re-emphasize Dr. Susan Jeffers book, you simply must *Feel the Fear and do it Anyways* - it's that simple. Take a break from busy and find the time to do so. I promise it will be worth your while.

P.S. It quite frankly doesn't matter whether you are good or bad at whatever you're taking on. That is so not the point. Just set the fear aside and move on anything new that presents itself to you or that you really want to do.

Let's focus here on the number two reason the *Busy Audit* revealed we don't make change. Time is a funny excuse as to why we can't change our lives. It is one of the only things all of us humans have the same amount of. So before you get mad and stop reading, I want to give you a quick snapshot of how you are currently spending your time, then you can make an informed decision as to whether you want to move your time around and give yourself to some areas in your life that may need a bit more of your time.

Shift Happens – A Snapshot of Your Life

Rank yourself in the following areas:

A = *Very Satisfied*

B = *Satisfied*

C = *Dissatisfied*

D = *Very Dissatisfied*

Health   A   B   C   D

	A	B	C	D
Health	A	B	C	D
Physical Activity	A	B	C	D
Your Body	A	B	C	D
Mental	A	B	C	D
Food and Nutrition	A	B	C	D
Career	A	B	C	D
Finances	A	B	C	D
Personal Development	A	B	C	D
Community Involvement	A	B	C	D
Relationships	A	B	C	D
Spirituality	A	B	C	D
Home	A	B	C	D
Play and Recreation	A	B	C	D

Once you have given all of these areas of your life a ranking, choose three that you know currently needs a little time and attention. Then, choose three areas in your life that you can extract a little time and attention. And for the next week, **do a time swap**.

It's not going to be easy at first, but just give it a try. This is one small change that can have huge results for you. Once we make small changes and get moving on areas in our lives that need momentum, that slow build will start to add up and big changes will just fall into place.

There is no need to over-think it all. What we have to do is use our mind as support systems to go within ourselves and find the real answers. Call it heart-based decision making, intuition, gut feelings, energetically driven, whatever works for you.

Bottom line for you over-thinkers: do your homework, but put a timeline on when a decision needs to be made and start making some changes. The more you practice this, the easier it will get.

There you have it, a way to conquer your fear, put time into perspective and tame your mind. Consider yourself now well equipped to take the leap.

CHAPTER 23

The Fearless Leap: Going After What We Really Want

Breaking Busy: To live in the life you truly want, clear
out clutter and welcome in clarity.

Question: What is one thing that you would like to change in your life right now, knowing that doing so would move you towards the life you truly want to be living?

This is the question I asked my readers last year and they came back full force with a variety of answers, which I have captured in eleven categories and themes (to follow shortly).

Through this research, what I found is that we feel like we are trapped in a "Cycle of Busy" because of our circumstances, debt and habits. What I really think we have done is slowly turned up the heat in the pot we all live in, fueled by racing technology, non-stop in-the-moment information and instant gratification, and have done so to a pace that is simply not sustainable. It's as if we are ticking time bombs waiting for the shoe to drop.

We have shaped our lives from the standpoint of "when this, then that, then I will…" I am here to tell you that you don't have to live your life walking around on eggshells, living how you think others want you to live or waiting for that magical "someday" when you can actually live the life you really want. It's time to take your life back. Today.

The rest of this book is for the twenty percent of you who are willing to mix things up - those of you who are open to making that gradual turn out of the "hover-lane." You're willing to try a new way of thinking as a test or on a trial basis. You have that "let's just see what happens" open-minded way of thinking. If nothing else, you can always go back to hovering once you've given the calm approach to life a test drive.

Just so we are clear, this is the section of the book where the proverbial rubber hits the road and some effort is going to be required. But not to worry, you can handle it.

So, back to the question at hand: What do we want to change?

One thousand people asked in the *Busy Audit*, top eleven answers on the board:

1. Get More Organized
2. Reduce Debt
3. Live Healthier
4. Stop Procrastinating
5. Reduce Stress
6. Get Rid of Negative People
7. Reduce Guilt
8. Increase Career/Job Satisfaction
9. Get to Know 'ME' Better
10. Find More Balance
11. Live from a Place of Kindness

Which of these themes hits home for you?

The good news is that taking the leap toward the life you really want isn't that hard once you make the decision to do so. We've already taken care of facing our fears and taming those overburdening thoughts in our minds, so we're well on our way. Now it's about gaining a real clear picture of where you want to be and taking the steps to get there.

In the most basic sense, what this research has told me is that the only way we will find clarity in our lives is if we reduce or eliminate the clutter. And so, over the next eleven chapters, you will have the opportunity to find your clarity while reducing your clutter, through each of the above top eleven themes that lead the charge for change, according to the survey results. So roll up your sleeves and let's get started.

**Clearing the Clutter
and Gaining Clarity**

CHAPTER 24

Change 1: The Organized Buy-In

Breaking Busy: While we can't avoid "stuff," we can organize it.

There is a lot of pressure to be organized in today's world, because as we as human race are growing and space is being pushed to its limits in most parts of the planet. The pressure is literally on. If you feel like you need more organization in your life, then you probably do. This, however, doesn't mean that you have to come to be just like your cubicle workmate, who's every pen and note is perfectly lined up by color and alphabetical sequence. Let's be real, that's not healthy either. Getting organized is a very personal decision.

My observation with the need to be organized, being the number one change that came out in the *Busy Audit* survey, is two-fold:

1. Some of us really do need to get organized.

2. The world judges us and we put pressure on ourselves to get organized. This was the highest ranked change that the people surveyed felt that they needed to make to get what they wanted in life. The question remains is this our personal judgment and pressure on ourselves or is it what we really need to do.

3. OR (option 3) is there a happy middle ground?

There is no overnight solution. This is a process that may take some time.

One place to start is where you live. Take an honest look at your home. Plan to only keep things that are useful and that energetically makes you happy. What I mean by this is that if it's an eyesore that makes you snarl every time you walk by, then it may be time to let it go. Think about getting rid of anything that doesn't serve a positive purpose in your life. These are *your* choices to make. You get to make your life whatever you want it to be. Free yourself from the clutter and open space to give the things that make you feel happy and light a more predominant place in your home.

Why do we all have so much stuff? I have asked this question hundreds of times to my audiences over the past twelve years. To really get people thinking about their answer, I ask, "If you had to evacuate your house, what would you want to take?" The response is always: photos.

So if it's just photos that are so important to us, why do I sit here with a drawer full of three half used rolls of masking tape, batteries that I'm not sure even work and a brimming box of straggly electronic wires for cameras, cell phones and other technological gadgetry that I'll probably never find the matching gadget for?

Don't we all have that drawer (or several of them)? Depending on how long you've lived in your present house, you've probably been tossing all kinds of things into your drawers, closets, storerooms, basements or attics over the months, years or decades. Maybe you've finally convinced yourself that you absolutely have to do some clearing out and organizing? Or maybe it's time to? There is such an amazing feeling you get when you get rid of stuff that you no longer use.

Start with just one little, useless thing. Just try it.

Here are some of my favorite tips to "Get Organized":

- Choose one tool and stick with it.
- Write "No Is An Option" at the top of your daily to-do list.
- Put "stuff" away now.
- Take control of your time, unapologetically.

- Simply have less "stuff."
- When you bring something into your house, get rid of something you no longer use.
- If you haven't touched it in six months, bid it farewell.
- Remember YOU control YOUR life.
- Tackle messes one room, drawer or closet at a time.
- Back up your files on your computer.
- Organize for tomorrow at the end of today.

CHAPTER 25

Change 2: Becoming Selectively Indebted

Breaking Busy: Talking money can be as tough as talking dirty.

Talking money requires the same skills and approaches at talking dirty. Because the second highest change most people would make in their lives is to reduce debt, it needs to be addressed with some actionable steps to help you get there. Much like sitting down to talk with your spouse or partner about sex, it takes a little courage.

When you carefully consider how difficult it is to talk about money, you will find that the same issues come up when we want and need to talk to our significant others about sex. For both conversations to happen, and to be authentic, we need to **trust** and **feel safe**. The rest is skills and details.

Let me know what you think.

I had to have those tough conversations this year, both with my husband *and* with myself. I'm coming up on my twentieth year of being in financial denial. I just have always thought that *everything will be OK.* And on the surface, it looked like it was. I had my office manager pay my company bills, credit cards, etc. I made a good salary as a speaker, so I basically just did what I wanted to and spent as I wanted to. Late last year, I had a small "get your shit together" moment and decided that I no longer wanted to live with my head in the sand. I took two weeks and opened the books. ALL of them. And let me tell you, the picture painted was not pretty. On the bright side, I had some great contracts moving into the next year and some savings I had accumulated for twenty years. However, most couples would go bankrupt with the amount of debt I had single-handedly piled up, but bankruptcy was not an option for me. I put it all on paper, talked to my bank manager and (at her advice) hired a Financial Success Coach. He got me in line pretty quick: making me look at the psychological side of money and what got me to that point in the first place.

#1. In order to truly find financial freedom, you have to drop your ego. Just like in the movie *Top Gun*, when Maverick is told that "his ego is cashing cheques that his butt can't afford." That was me.

Before I got to work on paying off the debt, I met with my Chartered Accountant and gave me a picture of how I was going to get to where I wanted to be. For three months, I promised myself that I would track everything I spent and check-in with my financial picture for ten to fifteen minutes a day. The deal was that I wasn't going to judge myself on what I was buying, but I did have to write it all down. That step alone was so empowering. I know it's been said thousands of times, but the freedom and power you feel when you become vulnerable and honest and to take the financial bull by the horns is amazing. I have become evangelistic about my enthusiasm for getting my "shift" together. Try it. It is so worth the risk.

#2. The next step is to bring your significant other into the picture. I wanted to get my husband to do the same thing as I was doing. Our history talking about money has almost always caused tension. So, I went looking for some advise and found *thesimpledollar.com*. With permission, I am listing their suggestions here.

Here are ten tips for getting the discussion started – and making sure that it doesn't devolve into an emotional battle.

1. Start off talking about goals. Ask your spouse when he/she wants to retire and what he/she wants to do after retirement. Ask what his/her dreams are – where would they like to be in five or ten years. The point is to think positively about money by asking where it can get you.

2. Admit your own mistakes. If you're having this discussion, it's likely you're not blameless. Start off by admitting your own mistakes. Before the discussion, evaluate your own spending and figure out where you've spent too much. For me, I admitted to spending too much on books and on eating out, both of which were seriously draining our finances.

3. Look your spouse right in the eye and hold their hand. No matter how big your spouse's mistakes are, never ever give any sign that you are anything other than compassionate and loving. For me, this meant that as my wife was summoning the courage to express her fears, her spending problems and her doubts, I sat next to her, looked right at her, listened attentively and placed my hand on top of hers. It was a simple gesture, but it reminded her of the love that we share.

4. Be goal-oriented. You're having this talk to achieve some sort of goal. Maybe you're realizing that credit card bills are getting too high or maybe you're starting to think about having children – or about life after the kids leave the nest. Let your partner know what the goal of the conversation is, but don't frame it around "you need to change your behavior." Be very specific about what you want to accomplish: "I would like to get these credit cards paid off" or "We're about to finish paying off the house and I'd like to think about an upgrade."

5. Look at numbers – but don't judge. When I did this, I let my wife see all of my statements first and gave her a pen to mark off anything she found questionable. She was so blown away by the openness that she almost automatically did the same thing once we evaluated my spending, without a peep. If I had started off by demanding her statements, then it would have turned into a giant war.

6. Be fair. If/when your spouse admits to overspending, don't blow up at them. *We live in a consumerist society that is designed to push our buttons and trick us into spending.* Even worse is that it's a pattern that's very difficult to break – it's a very socially acceptable addiction. Instead of exploding, ask them what they think of the spending: is it reasonable? Is it more important to them than paying off a credit card? **Do not** blow up if your spouse gives an answer that you don't like.

7. Create goals that you both agree on. Each of you should make a list of the goals you'd like to reach, both in the short term and in the long term. Then, find the ones that mesh together and agree to work towards them. For example, my wife and I are both interested in being debt free as soon as possible, buying a home in the near future and retiring early, so we've made that one of our primary goals. Now, we think of our spending in terms of these goals.

8. Create plans to reach those goals. For each of your common goals, spend some time figuring out how you can get there. Do you need to cut down on the Starbucks visits? Does your spouse need to spend less cash on authentic baseball jerseys (Hey, I've seen a couple where the husband was budgeting almost $10K on baseball-related apparel a year)? Each of you needs to be willing to make some sort of sacrifice to reach the goal and if you're initiating this, you should be the first one to offer up something.

9. Agree to talk about it regularly. I am a big fan of a monthly family meeting about money issues. This should include the children as early as possible. This way, all parties can stay on the ball and everyone can have a say in any planning decisions.

10. Do something romantic afterwards. After our first talk, I made dinner for the three of us while my wife picked up our son from daycare. After supper and some playtime, our child went to bed and we spent a romantic evening together to secure in the new bonds we had just built.

Adapted from Trent @ thesimpledollar.com

CHAPTER 26

Change 3: Increasing Fitness and Overall Health

Breaking Busy: When you feel like you've got nothing left in the tank, simply add oxygen.

Energy out = Energy in. I have spoken these words for years and to flip to how we fuel our bodies, you also need to say **Energy in = Energy out**. Quick science lesson: We know that our bodies are made mostly of water - hydrogen and oxygen, with oxygen holding the most mass of any component in our bodies. So, if we want to build strength and energy, what do we do? We fuel the greatest constituent of our bodies: oxygen.

The number one ingredient that will add vibrancy to your life that you must put into your system is oxygen and exercise does that for us. Living vibrantly well into our eighties and nineties requires circulation and that means moving your body. Whether you are a walker or a runner, a biker or a swimmer, practice yoga or garden, it's just a matter of getting more oxygen running through your body more often.

When it comes to exercise, there are two key tips that I can give you to get you moving:

1. We are exactly who we are because of our habits. So always **exercise on a Monday**. If we do something on a Monday, we tend to do something on a Wednesday and maybe even on a Thursday and Saturday. If an active Monday turns into an active Wednesday, then it most likely will turn into an energetic next week and so on.

2.   We over-think everything. It's not the exercise that is hard; it's getting *to the exercise* that is hard. So stop over-thinking it and start **the "Don't Think" method of exercise**. For example, you want to go for a brisk walk at lunch, but at the last minute your colleagues ask you to join them at this new restaurant. Start saying to yourself; "Don't think, don't think," put on your walking shoes and *don't think yourself* right out the door. We can find every reason on the planet to *not* move, but your long-term health is the most important reason *to* move. You will feel like you are one up on the world when you do. Every time you are presented with the option to either take the stairs versus the escalator or elevator, the choice is yours to make. When you get older, do you want to be dancing on a cruise ship or sitting in a care home? I know that sounds harsh, but it's the truth.

The great thing about the "Energy Out = Energy In" principle of exercise is that what exertion we make, comes back to us ten-fold. What's one of the worst feelings in our Busy Lives? When we are absolutely exhausted at the end of our rope and we have to meet yet another demand or deadline It can often feel like "Energy Out *without* any Energy In." Exercise is different. Energy Out by moving our bodies and getting active leads to Energy In, which fuels us to have even more gusto to take on our action-packed days. Oxygen people. Oxygen.

As we know, our long-term health is so much more than exercise (though that's a pretty big component in my world). But here's the good news: the other components of health, happiness, joy and self-esteem don't have to be complicated. They are all very achievable and cost virtually nothing, except a bit of your time. Yes, I hear you grumbling, but refer back to the *Snapshot of Your Life* Assessment at the beginning on Section 3 if you're still thinking "I don't *have* time." Sometimes we need to take time away from what is working to focus on what isn't working.

There are seven simple things we all need to do each day and I guarantee that by doing them, it will leave you feeling more settled, calm and like yourself. And for all you Type A, driven, self-confident people, let's make our goal this year to have our Self Esteem rise to meet our Self Confidence! Here are a few more tips that I like to call **A Mini Health BOOST for Busy People**:

1. Get some good **quality sleep each night**. According to experts, that means at least eight hours. No, I don't want to hear how you function well on five hours. Get eight!

2. **Eat healthy unprocessed foods daily.** This means more fruits and veggies every day…and then, throw one more portion in because we all know that you didn't get enough.

3. **Get some real fresh air each day**. Get outside for at least fifteen minutes, move and just BREATHE, even if it means parking across the lot to walk to the store. Fresh air, during daylight hours, is amazing for your personal sense of self. And if you can do it in nature, even better.

4. **Move your body** for at least ten minutes a day. Ask yourself, "What do you have in the tank today?" Then get moving. The endorphins allow you to be more of yourself and the mental and physical lift helps you to assist others with their journeys.

To take this a step further, make sure that you move at least ten minutes **in every hour**. Make you office less convenient, so that you have to at least stretch to get things. Put your garbage or recycling bin a short distance from your desk and create an enjoyable mindset about making a little lunge over to them. Set your coffee, water or phone on the table across the room, so that you have to get up to get them.

5. Have at least **one meaningful connection** with another person **each day**. We're not just talking about "Hi, how are you?" but something that is honest and transparent. I don't know about you, but I am just sick to death with pretentious chitchats. Maybe I'm getting too old for these types of B.S. conversations. Cut to the chase and be yourself. You might just learn something really cool.

6. **Laugh!** Even if it means finding an obscurity to laugh at, just laugh. Find your funny faster every day.

7. BONUS: If you get the chance, **reach out and do something that has no consequence to you**. Help someone, do something kind for a group of people, smile at someone you don't know. It's the "Give Factor."

CHAPTER 27

Change 4: Put-Offs Quickly Become Off-Putting

Breaking Busy: Instead of trying to stop procrastinating, we need to figure out how to do it
better.

According to Wikipedia, **Procrastination** is "the deferment or avoidance of an action or task and is often linked to perfectionism. For the person procrastinating, this may result in stress, a sense of guilt, the loss of productivity, the creation of crisis and the chagrin of others for not fulfilling one's responsibilities or commitments." While it is normal for individuals to procrastinate to some degree, it becomes a problem when it impedes normal functioning.

One of my favorite quotes comes from a great Canadian philosopher Steve Smith, aka Red Green, from a biography that was done on his life as a television star. He said, "Thank God we only have one hundred years to live. We procrastinate so much already, if we had more time, we'd get nothing done!"

We tend to feel that life is infinite and we keep putting things off. Or is it that we just don't want to do some of these things? It probably is a combination of several factors. Here's what I want to suggest: I want you to test your procrastination resistance and make a commitment publicly to act on all things that come to mind for one week. That means if a load of laundry comes out of the dryer, it has to be folded immediately and put it away as it is done. If you see a plant that needs water, jump on it right then. If there's dust on something you notice, use your sleeve to get it off. As mail comes into the office, open it and deal with each piece. Now, I don't know about you, but I'm starting to get a bit of a headache. I'll take some Advil right now. What's calling for your immediate attention?

When we think about procrastination, we try and figure out how to cure it. But let's be real; this is impossible. There is always an infinite number of things that you *could* be doing. No matter what you work on, you're not working on everything else. So the question is not how to avoid procrastination, but how to procrastinate well.

There are three kinds of procrastination - depending on what you do instead of working on something - you could work on:

1. Nothing

2. Something less important

3. Something more important.

Strategic procrastination is about the difference between big stuff and small stuff. Ask yourself what is small stuff or less important. As sad as it is to say, work has zero chance of being mentioned in your obituary. The flip side of this statement is: What it is that will turn out to be your best contribution? This may be the age-old question and the answer will probably continue to remain unclear as we all evolve. Let's start with the fact that you can safely rule out shaving, doing your laundry, organizing your knives and forks drawer, cleaning the house, writing thank-you notes, or some of my favorite ones: doing the cookie exchange, insisting that all holiday baking be done by you and anything that might be called an "errand." These are the clutter items we do to avoid doing something that will actually move us towards what we really want. Healthy procrastination is avoiding errands to do *real work*.

Real work needs two things errands don't: big chunks of time and the right mood. This is what I referred to in Section 2 as "Bubble time." You need to be mindful when you create your "Rockstar Day" formula. Here's my best example: I like to sell things before I have created them, like this book. I had a client who wants the book for an event, so I worked backwards. I needed ninety days from the event to have the book to my publisher and that gave me nine weeks to finish it. As a great procrastinator, I know I work well with deadlines. We all fill the time we are allotted. It's kind of like gravity; *it's the law.*

Here are a few questions you can ask yourself to figure out how you can become a more healthy procrastinator:

1. What are the most important problems in your work and home life?

2. Are you working on one of them?

3. Why not?

4. What's the best thing that you could be working on and why aren't you?

Most people will shy away from this last question in particular. I shy away from it myself. I see it there on the page and quickly move on to the next sentence. Please don't be like me. Take on the challenge of answering the question.

I recently interviewed one of my favorite people Colin Hiles. He is known as the "Midlife Maverick." He, like me, suggests that as adults, we look at and answer the question "What do we really want?" And we get very clear. What are you tolerating in your life? And highlight "tolerations." But what I want to emphasize from his interview is all the stuff we have on our plates to get done. When you look at all the "stuff" you "need to do," ask yourself: "Does this item/task energize me? Is it neutral to me, or is it an unenergetic task? Does it burn me out?" Eliminate all the things that burn you out. Move towards those things that energize you and only do a few things that are neutral. Then, procrastination won't be such a big issue for you.

The way to "solve" the problem of procrastination is to let delight pull you, instead of making a to-do list push you. Work on an ambitious project you really enjoy and sail as close to the wind as you can - you'll leave the right things undone.

CHAPTER 28

Change 5: Reducing Stress

Breaking Busy: Stressful situations aren't going to disappear, so we might as well figure out how to face them.

Stress is the body's reaction to any change that requires an adjustment or response. The body reacts to these changes with physical, mental and emotional responses. Stress is a normal part of life. Many events that happen to you and around you, as well as the many things that you do yourself, create stress. You can experience stress from your environment, your body and your thoughts.

The human body is designed to experience stress and react to it. Stress can be positive, keeping us alert and ready to avoid danger; it can also be not so positive. Stress becomes negative when a person faces continuous challenges without relief or relaxation between challenges. As a result, we become overworked and stress-related tension builds. And when that stress continues without relief, it can lead to a condition called distress. Distress can then lead to physical symptoms including headaches, upset stomach, elevated blood pressure, chest pain and problems sleeping. Research suggests that stress also can bring on or worsen certain symptoms or diseases.

It's no surprise that stress has become the number one agent of disease in the world. It causes inflammation and all diseases grow and thrive anywhere in the body where inflammation is.

According to WebMD:

- Seventy-five percent to ninety percent of all doctor's office visits are for stress-related ailments and complaints.

- Stress can play a part in problems such as headaches, high blood pressure, heart problems, diabetes, skin conditions, asthma, arthritis, depression and anxiety.
- The Occupational Safety and Health Administration (OSHA) declared stress a hazard of the workplace. Stress costs North American industry more than $300 billion annually.

Most of us know and have heard similar stress statistics for years. And depending on how your body reacts to your daily stresses, these points may really hit home. How accustom we are to stress and how we deal with it often dictates what we do to relive stresses.

Some of us who have highly stressful jobs seem to fare well and don't allow stresses to wreak havoc in our bodies; while others who seemingly have low stress lives, get very stressed over smaller issues. One piece of research I found years ago in the *Journal of Medicine* suggested that we have change/stress resilient personalities. This study found that people with high levels of stress, but low levels of illness, share three characteristics, which are sometimes referred to as the three "C's". Stress-resistant personalities have:

- **Control** – a sense of purpose and direction in their life.
- **Commitment** – to work, hobbies, social life or family.
- **Challenge** – seeing changes in life as normal and positive rather than as a threat.

However, not everyone is born with these characteristics, and may people have to relearn specific life skills in areas such as assertiveness or rational thinking to better equip them to cope with the demands of everyday life.

Here are just a few simple tips to de-stress and to lower the inflammation in your body caused by stress. Our health is at stake and life is not going to slow down. This is about YOU **Finding Peace in the Chaos**.

1. **Stop feeding the inflammation**. This is done by reducing all sugar and starchy foods. If you need to get started, just have a sugar-free day and build up from there. Then, try and link four to six of those days in a row.

2. Take a deep breath. Hold it for a moment and then, exhale. Feel more relaxed? Breathing exercises, like the ones taught in yoga classes, is one way to relax. Learn about different ways to relax your mind and body. Being relaxed can help ease stress; it can also relieve anxiety, depression and sleep problems, which are all aggravated by stress.

3. **Relax**. Calm the mind, the body, or even better, both. Relaxing can quiet your mind and make you feel peaceful and calm. Your body also reacts when you relax. For example, your muscles may be less tense and more flexible. I know I have said it before, but this is where Yoga is amazing. Note: You do not need to be in a gym wearing those oh-so-cute clothes that are only made for size zero to six people. There is ample Yoga online and bonus - it's free. Take a chance and try an online class at home today.

There are different ways to relax. You may find one or more ways to help calm you down and feel at peace. Maybe it's spending time in your bathtub with candles and Epsom salts or maybe you created a space in your home that is just yours, in a chair or in your office, surrounded by all the things you love and cherish. Your space is where you can read for pleasure, nap for relaxation or mediate and quiet your mind.

4. **Change your mind and make the time**. You deserve some distressing time. If you have to get up twenty minutes before everyone else in your home wakes up or stay up thirty minutes after they've all gone to bed, then try it. It's up to you. Just take action, in any form, and create your own stress-reducing program.

Stress is always going to be a part of our lives. We get to decide how much we internalize it and allow it to affect our health or how much we make time to balance it out by growing the peace and relaxation in our lives.

CHAPTER 29

Change 6: Cutting Back on Negative Influences in Your Life

Breaking Busy: If there's negativity in your life that isn't serving you, face it with compassion, or freely let it go.

When my girls were just born, I taught at my local Community College. I led a sixteen-week program for marginalized women who were trying to get their lives back on track. The most common characteristics amongst these women was that most of them had dropped out of high school and nearly sixty percent of them had their first child in their late teens. Needless to say, many of them did not grow up in highly supportive, life-nourishing families. Most of these women were also in negative relationships.

Ironically, before my first day of classes, one of my colleagues told me that most of the women in my class would not be in the same relationships by the end of the sixteen-week program. She was right. I ended up using my husband's truck to move many of those women and their kids out of these 'not so great' home environments. Why? Because they were ready to move on. They were ready to create better lives for themselves. They chose to take a long hard look at their relationships, deciding if the negativity was something that could be faced with compassion or if it was simply a weight that would be forever bearing them down, keeping them from freely progressing into the life they truly desired. In the end, most of these women made their choice.

First and foremost, it's important to recognize when we have negative people and influences in our lives that the motivation behind someone who is negative is not always a conscious attempt to *be negative*. When you start to move forward in your life, making improvements within yourself, those around us, who are not self-aware, will subconsciously do and say things to try and keep you from changing. If you change and they don't, they may have to change too…and as we've learned, change is scary.

With that being said, here are some warning signs and characteristics of people who tend to be negative:

Negative people tend to:

- Be fearful and afraid of what is happening in the news, economy and society.
- Always seem bored. There is never enough action going on around them.
- Have a negative identity about themselves.
- Enjoy picking fights with you and most people around them. They enjoy the adrenaline rush they get from getting mad at people.
- Tend to be critical and paranoid that everyone and everything is always out to get them. There is always something wrong. They never seem to catch a break.
- Will only do things that will give them personal gain.
- Are seldom grateful about anything.
- Live with low-level anxiety all the time.
- Blame their parents or others for how they have turned out.
- Don't enjoy life's little pleasures, food, smell of rain in the spring, the warmth of sun on their skins, etc.
- Tend to have unrealistic glorification of their past (i.e. the good ol' days).

If you feel like you are being held back by negative influences that are keeping you from making the changes you want to make to move forward in your life, you basically have three choices:

1. Do nothing and muddle through moving forward.

2. If the relationship means anything to you and you want to preserve it, bring these negative behaviors and mindsets to the awareness of these negative people in your life in a respectable way.

3. If you don't care to maintain the relationship, then simply move on. Get rid of this relationship in your life. If you don't, you will have a very tough time becoming who you want to become and finding clarity, peace and happiness will be almost impossible. Once again, our choice what we will do. Just give yourself permission to become who you want to be.

Negative people and influences, like stress and will always exist. So too will our choice about what we choose to do about them.

CHAPTER 30

Change 7: Throwing Guilt Down the Gutter: You Might be a Martyr if…

Breaking Busy: Guilt and Martyrdom are no longer in vogue.

Guilt, as defined by Webster's New World Dictionary is "The fact of doing something wrong or committing an offence. A feeling of self-reproach from believing one has done something wrong."

OK, so if you in fact have done something wrong, you should feel some guilt. Interesting point here is that the word "guilt" falls between the words "guillotine" and "Guinea pig" – both of which can also serve to keep us in line.

Over the years, the emotion of guilt has served the human race well in modifying our behaviors. Most of the world has one scary thing in common: we all seem to buy into the idea that we should be feeling some guilt, for one reason or another. And if you are not really feeling any guilt, well then, you should probably be feeling guilty about the fact that you are not. Perhaps you missed one person on your Christmas card list and you still haven't forgiven yourself, even several months into the new year. (Extra guilt if they sent *you* a card.) Maybe you just couldn't bring yourself to fight those parking lot crowds to find the latest electronic I-something for one of your kids. (Because we all know that last year's model just doesn't cut it.) You decided to go out and buy some goodies for your kids' school party, instead of baking them yourself this year. God forbid! What would Martha think? And the list goes on.

The Martyr has been around for centuries and I think it is high time we declared an epidemic on this once revered personal characteristic. Before I squash the glorious limelight of the Martyr, let me just say that it does give us a great training background for a career as a soap star.

Here are some of the humorous lines I wrote back in the 90s, when I wrote *You Might be a Martyr*. See if any fit for you.

...if going to the bathroom with the door closed is considered pampering yourself – you might be a Martyr.

...if joining a twelve step program is not appealing to you because there are not enough steps – you might be a Martyr.

...if your "Out Basket" has turned into a second "In Basket" – you might be a Martyr.

...if you have not discovered the word "NO" yet – you might be a Martyr.

...if dinner out involves going through a drive through – you might be a Martyr.

...if you are using your calendar to schedule your love life – you might be a Martyr.

Whoever said you are only a good person if you give so much of yourself that there is nothing left to drag into the shower every morning? That point when you've become too tired to even think about it.

So here is the challenge as we try to move forward in our pursuit of Peace in the Chaos in today's world: **Find some balance**. It's that simple and that hard all at the same time. Bottom line: you will be living *YOUR* life when you move towards creating balance. And by the way, "Balance" is how *You and only You* define it. No single book or person is going to give you the answer to steer you from guilt and martyrdom to peace and calm. If you are working towards balance in your life, the fact that you have chosen to do so will decrease your feeling of guilt.

Here's the Balance Secrete: there is NO such thing as balance. If you work inside or outside of your home, excluding sleeping, you spend two thirds of your life working, so it's not balanced to begin with. The question then becomes what you do to make the most out of that other one third.

The number one thing you can do to increase a feeling of balance in your work and home life is to start making a decisions based on your true core values. Linda Duxbury from Carlton University has done extensive research in the area of Work-Life Balance. Her findings prove that those of us who simply sense some control over when and where we work have more balance in our lives. When we do, we experience more job satisfaction, less absenteeism, stress leave and mental health days off. A sense of harmony or peace comes from choosing to do things with your free time that fulfills and nourishes your soul and aligns with your values.

This is not Einstein-level stuff here. Moving towards a "balanced life" is a continuing process. It will change as you, your family, the weather and the moon changes. As you get comfortable getting back to eating less sugar and getting back into the norm of the day-to-day, your boss might throw you a project that you did not expected, you may get transferred, a family member may turn ill, or any other form of the unexpected lands at your door…and off you go on the roller coaster again. That's the deal. That's Life. We either fight against it or roll with it.

The good news is that when life seems unbalanced and chaotic, it will all change, and then, it will all change once again. There's really no point in trying to predict life. All we can do is create balance and embrace what comes our way. As one of my favorite Nike posters says: "There is No Finish Line."

When you think about it, how do we ever have time to feel guilt? Chaos, the unexpected, stress, working past negative influences, and oh ya, Busyness. But we seem to find the time. So, don't dwell on what you could have, should have or didn't do - just keep it all in perspective. If you feel so wholly overwhelmed, just go and get yourself one of those SAD lights, pour yourself a tall glass of chardonnay and just sit back, absorb the light, make like you're sitting on a sandy beach and wait for the guilt to melt away.

Life Perspectives to Reduce Your Guilt

- No matter how good you have it, someone has it better than you.

- Someone has to take the last piece and it should be you. Now the dish can be washed.

- Sending your cards late is a great marketing strategy. You stand out from the crowd.

- If you take a nap now, then you will have more energy for tonight.

- Life is uncertain, eat dessert first.

- You deserve a break today, Ronald McDonald said so, and who's going to argue with a tall red head?

- Homework kills trees; stop the madness! (This one my daughter gave me.)

- Always put your best foot forward and you should be in great shoes.

- Mom said I should always wear nice underwear. Stop by to see Victoria Secret, but just stay away from the 10x10 foot screen television showcasing the latest VS fashion show. It's not much of an esteem builder.

- Dinner out once a week is an ideal way to get new recipes for your family.

- You bought your "made from scratch" pie from the bakery and put it in your own pie dish. Hey, *someone* made it from scratch! (If this idea doesn't work, my thought is that if you made the money that paid for that pie, you made that PIE!)

- All that canning in the fall takes so much time away from the kids.

- All that "stuff" you bought this year is really helping to boost the economy.

Reducing guilt is just how you choose to look at things. Make this week a "Guilt Free Zone Week."

CHAPTER 31

Change 8: What To Do When Satisfaction Isn't Guaranteed

Breaking Busy: To increase satisfaction in your job, increase it outside of your job.

We need to get clear on one fact. Our job's job is to not have to be "the be-all to end all" for our self-worth and personal satisfaction. Our entire identity is not supposed to come solely out of our careers. Our jobs don't define us; they are simply extensions of who we are. It's our own "job" to create our self-worth and satisfaction because the only place we're going to truly find it is inside of ourselves. External satisfaction is never guaranteed.

As we talked about in the last chapter, we will spend two thirds of our lives working. So if that is the case, what do we do to be the best version of ourselves in our day-to-day careers? One thing I know is that most of the planet is not making work out of their purpose; but that doesn't mean you shouldn't be able to express what your purpose is through your work. Here's an example: if you are a creative person and there is nothing in your work that allows you to express that creative side of you, then you are slowly killing your soul through your work. So what do you do? You would want to find other creative challenges within the workplace, perhaps find another workplace altogether where you can express yourself or maybe find an outlet outside of work that allows for your full creative expression.

Here's an interesting correlated fact: most of us are fairly accountable within our work because there are parameters we can get our heads around when it comes to accountability. Where we have dropped the ball is being accountable outside of our work. We don't do the things we love to do outside of work mostly because we have created this crazy "Busy Life". What I have found over the past twelve years of encouraging my participants to becoming more accountable in their home lives is that as they do so, they start to see their work differently. They get re-energized for the careers they have chosen. It's really quite simple: become accountable outside of your work life and your passion for work will improve. It's about giving yourself permission to take it back. To take back your life, that is.

When I wrote "Simple truths about getting a life" in *Shift…Or Get Off the Pot*, I knew that the most important thing was to get people moving on anything that would cause inertia to happen. It's simple physics: once you start moving, it's easier to stay in motion in that direction. On the very first page of *Shift*, I wrote, "Go directly to page 129 and answer the question there. When you have, come back and start the book.", because I knew that the energy that would be put into the question would start inertia moving. That one question bears repeating here:

"If you were just given two extra hours in a day, and the time's not being taken away from anything else, it's a gift and you cannot do *anything* that is job or career related, what would you want to do with that time?" There's the question. Write a few things down and **choose one** that you will **act on** over the next twenty-four hours. When you act on it, it will cause a reaction and you will start to see your work differently. I guarantee it.

You don't have to finish this "thing" you've chosen to do; you just have to get started. Breathe in deep and then back out and hold that item in your mind.

The final piece of the puzzle to increasing your job and career satisfaction is that you have to contact me with what you did or did not do in the next twenty-four hours. Share it either on Facebook (lindaedgecombe), Twitter (lindaedgecombe) or email (info@lindaedgecombe.com). Trust me on this one. It's a small, but very powerful gesture.

CHAPTER 32

Change 9: Balanced Living: The Classic Dilemma Between the Head and the Heart

Breaking Busy: It takes the differences of the head and
heart to make great decisions.

When I wrote *Shift...Or Get off the Pot,* I initially thought about calling the book *Make a Decision Already!* As we've covered, most of the planet hovers because where we are seems to be just fine. "Fine" is nothing other than a non-descript word that keeps us planted right where we are. As you move through this book, let's take this opportunity to practice thinking with our heads, listening to our hearts and becoming more aware of the value of our decisions made from within.

Balance is about allowing all of the parts of ourselves to peacefully work together, our hearts talk to our guts, our guts talk to our minds and our mind is at peace with our hearts and guts, even if what they say doesn't seem totally practical. Well, at least that's the ideal, but let's be real. The same voice in your mind that tells you to take an action is the same voice that usually ridicules you later for making that choice. Unfortunately, it's typical in our society to feel a conflict between what we want to do (our heart) and what we feel is practical (our mind). We end up living one third of our lives in a cubicle for the "benefits." We stay friends with people we only *kind of* like. We do and say things to fit in and seem cool, when those actions and words really go against what we feel is right in our hearts. Is your heart at fault? Are your feelings just silly and frivolous? Or maybe it's your mind that is to blame?

It might seem as though our minds are always coming up with conflicting messages and on it goes from there. We never really seem to "get out of it" and onto the messages of our hearts. We're subject to a lot of social conditioning that covers up and obscures our decisions and thoughts. Even if you really feel like you've made the right choice, how do you know for sure? How do you know it's not just what you think you *should* do?

I've created three keys to balancing the heart and mind. Here they are:

1. Avoid confusing the purpose of the heart and mind. The main reason we suffer from this illness of indecision is that we've confused the purpose of heart with that of the mind. The heart is like a compass - its purpose is to guide the direction our lives should take. Our heart takes a bird's eye view on our life and says, "This is where you are and this is the direction you need to go." Our mind, on the other hand, isn't designed for making value-driven decisions. The nature of the mind is one of conceptualizing, organizing and comparing information. It does this as best it can and says, "Here are the facts. Here are both sides of the story."

2. Think about each of your decisions. When deciding what phone to get, who to marry or whether you want to stay at your current job, we need the input of both our hearts and minds. Here's a potential flow of the decision-making process:

- **Gain information.** What is the implied benefit of the decision? Will it be something you'll regret? Although your mind may be telling you that the temporary benefit of a bad decision will be a wise one, in your heart you may still know that it's not the best thing to do. Seek information about it through your heart and evaluate in your mind.

- **Identify problems**. What might go wrong? Will you feel good after making the decision?

- **Explore options**. Think about what's best for you. Most of the time, doing what your heart tells you to do is the best choice.

- **Implement a plan and make a choice**. Learn from your mistakes and try, try again.

Doing this due diligence, especially on big decisions, takes any remorse away once the decision is made. Trust yourself once you have put this time in. By listening to your heart, you can train your mind to think like your heart, and eventually, you'll get them to work in harmony.

3. Keep practicing to fall into this new habit. Have you ever wondered how to tell whether a decision is right? It seems so difficult, doesn't it? But it becomes so easy when you think, "Is this choice going *with me*, or *against me?*" By asking that question, you'll find that the right choice is immediately evident. Learn to practice this every time you make a choice today. Just try it out. For one day, practice making all your decisions based on "Is this decision going with me or against me?" Go with yourself.

What's the Value of Knowing your Values?

The good news is that you can change everything about how you make decisions and balance your heart and mind by getting in touch with your core values. Balance, fulfillment and joy lives on the other side of the discovery of your values and their integration into your decision-making. By investing time and energy to get clear on your values, by defining and articulating what you really want from all areas of your life and by letting your values govern your decisions, you will live a fulfilling life. Yes, it's that simple.

Stepping out of "Busy Lane" is as easy, and as difficult, as getting clear on what has meaning for you and what needs to naturally fall off your plate. There doesn't have to be any strain to the decisions that you need to make to get you there; just let the balance of your heart and mind guide you.

To get to that point, here are Four Simple Steps to find balance and reduce "Busy," which I like to call **What do you hold in High Esteem?**

Step 1 – Take out your journal or a blank piece of paper. Open up your computer and Google the word "values." Find a site that most likely will have hundreds of words that represent potential values. Then, answer this question: "What in life is most important to me?" Write down whatever comes into you head. A little tip here is to not make any judgments at this stage. Just write *everything* down, no matter how weird, strange, amusing or scary! Try to find and write down about **twenty** values that mean a lot to you.

Step 2 – Look at your list. I want you to group your list of values into those that fall into similar categories. Now take however many values you have and pull out the **five** most important values for you today. Now, write them out again. It may sound redundant, but the power in this short exercise is in the pen; so please just humor here and write them out again. Now, look at your top five and pull out the **three** most important values. Write those three down in order of importance, leaving some space between each one as you write them on the page again.

Step 3 – For each of your top three values, I want you to write out **why** that value is important to you. Use some descriptive words and add some emotions to your descriptions. Look for what triggers a very strong emotion in you (joy, anger, love, hate, jealousy); there will probably be a link to a core value wrapped up there. For example, you may ask, "What does health mean to me?" To which the answer could be energy, travel, security, freedom, more quality time with my kids, etc etc. By answering this second question, you uncover your **core or underlying value**. In this example, health means you build the energy to truly enjoy your family and to see the world. Adventure and freedom are the core values. This is often a difficult question to answer because all of our values are important. Push yourself to choose and put the one you're letting go off to the side. Keep asking this question until you're left with your **most important value**. Write those ones on a sticky note or in your journal and your calendar, if you still use one. They should be big enough so that you can see them from across the other side of the room.

Step 4 – Rewrite your top three values. Your first assignment using these is to test your values. For one day, **tomorrow**, I want you to make **every decision** that comes across your plate **based on your core values** - where you go for lunch, what you wear, where you buy groceries, what you eat, who you spend time with after work, etc. Every decision. When you accept only the best, that's often what you get and the rest just falls by the wayside. This is the single most effective way to find balance and shift away from the busy life you have created. Instead of living your life like a racket ball game, responding to wherever the ball is going, you now get to decide how, where and if you even go after the ball. I guarantee you that the weight you are feeling on your shoulders is going to lift.

If you do nothing else with this book, other than practice value-based decision-making, your life will be forever changed. Keep me posted on your experience.

info@lindaedgecombe.com

CHAPTER 33

Change 10: Self-Awareness: Getting to Know Me Better

Breaking Busy: Fortune favors the self-aware.

I have said to my audiences many times that the most successful people I have ever come across are folks who are very self-aware. They are people who continuously "Notice what they notice." They know what their strengths are and they certainly know their weaknesses; they're okay to admit and face them all. Instead of just reacting to situations that happen to them, they ask themselves, "Why is that bugging me?" or, "Why am I so drawn to that person?" They have become fully aware of what pushes their buttons *and* what brings them joy; they're continuously curious as to *why*. We all need to have more wonder about how and why life unfolds as it does. What is your place in the world as it turns in our giant galaxy?

Here are some *Simple Steps* to help you get to know you better:

- Take some time to allow your mind to be quiet.

- Walk in nature and slow down your heart rate. Notice how you feel.

- When you have a decision to make, think about your options and breathe into the option. Notice whether the answer energizes you or causes a tightening in your body. This step will teach you to trust your gut and heart more. The more relaxed response is always the way of your heart and gut.

- Before you go to sleep at night, ask your soul a question. See if you wake with a few answers.

- Take a simple personality profile and find out your preferences. It's fun to see how your personality sees the world.

- Distinguish your thoughts and goals from other people's thoughts and goals.

Remember: Confidence and Courage *do not come before* you try something new. They come *after* you've gone through it. So put on your big pants (or big shoes) and move forward. That's where you learn about yourself.

So, you're spending time with you and building your self-awareness and esteem. The next question is, "Do you want to get Lucky?"

I recently spoke at an event and before I got up for my presentation, I had the pleasure of listening to Ross McBride. He spoke about Leadership and ended his presentation with some tips on how to be and find more luck in your life. He referred to some research done by a Professor of Psychology at the University of Hertfordshire in England. Richard Wiseman declares that he can help you find more luck in your life. He claims that there are folks who definitely are more lucky and successful and that they, like their lucky friends and coworkers, actually consistently practice what he calls "lucky behaviors." Even though, at first glance, Wiseman's Four Principles seem like some polished renditions of age-old "power of positive thinking" philosophies, they round out to some undeniable truths. For example, he says that lucky people tend to turn all bad luck into good. The lucky he says, also "expect good fortune," which makes sense. What Wiseman found is that lucky people are particularly open to possibility.

Why is it that some people always find fortune? It's not just dumb luck. Unlike the masses, lucky people are just more open to what is around them. And not only are they open to it, they are hardwired to notice the opportunities that present themselves. They are more awake in the moments of their lives.

There is distinct difference between "chance" and "luck." For example, if you win the lottery, that is a chance event. Yes, you did go out and purchase a ticket; but other than that, you have no control over the event. Wiseman claims that when people consistently experience good fortune, then by his definition, it is because of something they are *doing*. In other words, they **make their own luck**.

Here are some ways that lucky people think differently and practice lucky behaviors than those of unlucky people:

1. They are open to new experiences. Unlucky people are stuck in routines. Lucky people always want to try something new. Have you seen the movie *Yes Man* with Jim Carey? When Carey's character starts to say "Yes" to every opportunity that comes his way, his life really starts to pick up. (Very funny movie by the way.)

Ways to stay open:

- Strike up conversations with people who you encounter. Be the one to break the ice.

- After you meet someone interesting, follow up with them, but keep it light and stay relaxed.

- Smile more. People will want to meet you and will think that you are a nice person.

Instead of being laser-focused on your goals, open up a bit and you will catch more opportunities. Always have a few game plans in your head and leave room on that to-do list for possibility. Vary your routines continuously. Mix things up: where you go for coffee, have lunch etc. You will meet more people that way.

2. Maximize chance opportunities. Lucky people are skilled at creating, noticing and acting upon chance opportunities. They do this by building and maintaining strong networks, adopting a relaxed attitude to life and being open. Listen to your hunches and take note of nagging red flags.

3. Believe in lucky charms. When you see them, you will think something good is going to happen and those thoughts have power.

4.   **Listen to you lucky hunches**. Lucky people consistently make effective decision by listening to their intuition and gut feelings; they do things to sharpen their intuitive abilities. For example, by meditating and clearing their minds of cluttering thoughts, they can better hear that guiding voice from within them.

5.   **Expect good fortune.** Lucky people expect that their future is going to be bright and over time, that expectation becomes a self-fulfilling prophecy because they persist in the face of failure by shaping how they interact with other people.

OK, so the challenge here is to practice these behaviors for a few weeks and experience firsthand how your luck picks up. Keep me posted!

info@lindaedgecombe.com

CHAPTER 34

Change 11: Why Kindness is Highly Underrated

Breaking Busy: When in doubt (or chaos), be kind.

Several times in this book, I have revealed that the past few years have been the most challenging in my life. So my acute awareness of myself is front and center almost hourly. I have been working hard to stay in the moment, conscious and aware.

A few weeks ago, I was driving up the mountain to where I live and several cars had stopped in front of me. Then, I saw why. A turtle was crossing to make it to the other side of the road where the pond was. He made it to the other side and then, couldn't get up on the curb. And when he tried, he flipped on his back. All I could remember from science class was that turtles can't turn themselves over. So I jumped out of my car, ran across the street and turned him over and put him up on the grass. Several cars honked in approval. I felt this huge boost of what I called my "joy shot." It just felt so great to do something for someone or something. It felt good to be kind.

Kindness is usually more for us (the doer) than it even is for the person we are doing the kind act for. It doesn't matter how grim or chaotic our lives seem. Trust me when I say that the simplest act of kindness can put everything in perspective. Look for an opportunity to boost your joy today.

Learning to live from a place of kindness, both toward yourself and others, is one of the most underrated ways to break the cycles of our busy ways. I feel the best way to share some thoughts on kindness is to listen to the masters. I hope you enjoy these as much as I do. (This first one is for you to start being kinder to yourself.)

"Love and treat yourself, like you loved your children's baby toes."
~ Unknown

"It's also selfish because it makes you feel good when you help others. I've been helped by acts of kindness from strangers. That's why we're here, after all, to help others."
~ Carol Burnett

"Too often we underestimate the power of a touch, a smile, a kind word, a listening ear, an honest compliment, or the smallest act of caring, all of which have the potential to turn a life around."
~ Leo Buscaglia

"Kindness is more important than wisdom, and the recognition of this is the beginning of wisdom."
~ Theodore Isaac Rubin

"No kind action ever stops with itself. One kind action leads to another. Good example is followed. A single act of kindness throws out roots in all directions, and the roots spring up and make new trees."
~ Amelia Earhart

"If you haven't any charity in your heart, you have the worst kind of heart trouble."
~ Bob Hope

"For beautiful eyes, look for the good in others; for beautiful lips, speak only words of kindness; and for poise, walk with the knowledge that you are never alone."
~ Audrey Hepburn

"The end result of kindness is that it draws people to you."
~ Anita Roddick

"How beautiful a day can be when kindness touches it!"
~ George Elliston

"We make a living by what we get, but we make a life by what we give."
~ Winston Churchill

CHAPTER 35

Finding Peace in the Chaos

Breaking Busy: We chose Busy, now let's choose Peace.

You have known this all along: all you need to be creating and be living **the life you REALLY want** is already within you. Your power comes from everything you do and that is rooted in your heart. Love is your strongest power. Living wholeheartedly means loving yourself and giving that love and energy out to the world. It is boundless and abundant. What you give out will come back to you in ways you never imagined possible. In the powerful words of the Beatles, *"Love, Love, Love. Love is all you need."*

The chaos we have and are currently experiencing in our "Busy Lives" is there because we have **lost ourselves**. It's just stuff that's in the way of you seeing who you really are and keeps us from clearing it up. What we're looking for -peace, calm, happiness and purpose - has always been within us; we just have to clear the clutter to reveal it.

Our power to love, give and create is a power we all have. You *know* it. You *are* it. Now, you just have to start *believing it* again. I call this **remembering what you already know.**

Start to re-frame how you see your life and when you hit a road bump, don't look at it like a stumbling block. See it as just a new learning experience. When you start to feel overwhelmed by the "Busyness" of it all, take a moment and clear out some of the clutter. The gems are always there; they might just be sitting under ten feet of paper and a junk drawer full of old gadget charges.

If you want to find more peace in the chaos, start by giving more today. Give more of your time, love, energy, kindness, the best of you, all of your gifts. You might think that it sounds crazy to give more of yourself when you already feel exhausted, but remember what we talked about: make your decisions with care, balancing your heart and mind. When you do, those choices to give yourself will invigorate you, not drain you. Trust me. It's in that giving that will create the space and draw all that is good and desirable to you.

I was once having an educated argument with a Baptist Pastor friend of mine. His closing and very convincing point was, "Let's say all that we believe is made up. What's so wrong with living a life that is full of generosity, caring and kindness towards each other and the world we live in?"

"Great point," I thought.

The truth is, you will pull all the riches that life has to offer towards yourself by simply being yourself. This is the only purpose of life. Be who you were meant to be and give yourself to every aspect of your life. When you do, every choice, action and moment will no longer feel like a myriad of Busyness; it will all feel like a beautiful balance, fused with playfulness, laughter and calm.

To re-cap and emphasize why I decided to write this book; I asked my readers, 'If you could change one thing about yourself that you know would get you closer to what your Really Want', this is what they said:

One thousand people asked in the Busy Audit, top eleven answers on the board:

1. Get More Organized
2. Reduce Debt
3. Live Healthier
4. Stop Procrastinating
5. Reduce Stress
6. Get Rid of Negative People
7. Reduce Guilt

8. Increase Career/Job Satisfaction

9. Get to Know 'ME' Better

10. Find More Balance

11. Live from a Place of Kindness

Love yourself enough to just get started on one of them.

Clarity, peace and the real you await. How will you bring yourself to life today?

ABOUT AUTHOR

Linda Edgecombe is a Re-invention Strategist, motivational coach and engagement expert.

Linda is an internationally renowned, award-winning, celebrity speaker. Just inducted into the Speaker Hall of Fame, She is A mother of 2 and wife of one. Featured in the **Wall Street Journal as an Expert in Shifting Peoples Perspectives on their work and home life**.

She is an author of several books and has been invited to speak across the globe, inspiring people to simply "choose a slice of the planet". Most recently, she was presented with the Humanitarian of the Year Award, from the Women of Worth Foundation. And just this past August she came in second in the "North America's Next Greatest Speaker" contest. Not that she's bitter....

Linda's message is as welcome as a good belly laugh and as profound as an honest look in the mirror.

For more information on Linda's programs and publications

Check her out online at www.lindaedgecombe.com

Send her a note at info@lindaedgecombe.com

Receive her weekly 'kick in the butt' at

http://www.lindaedgecombe.com/newsletter-signup/

Like her on Facebook linda.edgecombe1

Try something old school and call her office 1-888-868-9601

CPSIA information can be obtained
at www.ICGtesting.com
Printed in the USA
LVOW13s1030290617
539734LV00012B/92/P